Step by Step
with
Richard Hughes

Clever cooking

in simple stages

Step by Step with Richard Hughes
Clever cooking in simple stages

Recipes compiled by
Richard Hughes

Photography by
Keiron Tovell
www.keirontovell.com

Written and edited by
Carolyn Bowden
carolynbowden@btinternet.com

Richard Hughes' Restaurants Ltd:-

The Lavender House Restaurant & Cookery School
39 The Street, Brundall, Norfolk, NR13 5AA
Tel: 01603 712215
www.thelavenderhouse.co.uk

Anna Sewell House Restaurant
26 Church Plain, Great Yarmouth, Norfolk, NR30 1NE
Tel: 01493 856859
www.annasewellhouserestaurant.co.uk

The Pigs
Norwich Road, Edgefield, Holt, Norfolk, NR24 2RL
Tel: 01263 587634
www.thepigs.org.uk
(Owned by Richard Hughes and Iain Wilson)

Also recommended:-

Byfords Café, Deli and Posh B&B
1-3 Shirehall Plain, Holt, Norfolk, NR25 6BG
Tel: 01263 711400
www.byfords.org.uk

The King's Head
19 High Street, Holt, Norfolk, NR25 6BN
Tel: 01263 712543

ISBN No. 978-0-9547636-3-3

By Appointment to
Her Majesty The Queen
Commercial Artists & Illustrators
Farrows Ltd
Norwich

Designed by Darrell Kennett, Sarah Batch and Patrick Currie at design agency Farrows who have been creating ideas for 29 years and still retain their first client to this day. Contact them at: www.farrows.co.uk

Printed by
Norwich Colour Print
www.norwichcolour.co.uk

FSC Mixed Sources
Product group from well-managed forests and other controlled sources
www.fsc.org Cert no. TT-COC-002425
© 1996 Forest Stewardship Council

It seems that everyone's interested in food these days. You only have to turn on the TV to find a cookery show, whether it's a well-known television personality trying out another country's cuisine, a top chef demonstrating a range of dishes, or a group of panellists trying to rustle up a meal in a matter of minutes. And if you flick through a newspaper or magazine, particularly the Sunday supplements, you'll find all sorts of ideas for eating out as well as for cooking for friends and family at home. In fact, we've all gone food mad, and I think we're the better for it; it's wonderful that so many people have woken up to the fact that we've got such fantastic produce on our doorstep.

At The Lavender House Restaurant & Cookery School in Brundall and our other restaurants, the Anna Sewell House Restaurant in Great Yarmouth, and The Pigs pub in Edgefield, we're

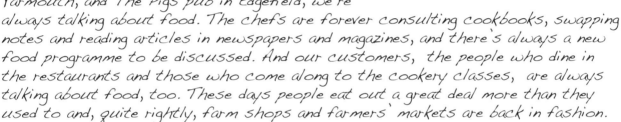

always talking about food. The chefs are forever consulting cookbooks, swapping notes and reading articles in newspapers and magazines, and there's always a new food programme to be discussed. And our customers, the people who dine in the restaurants and those who come along to the cookery classes, are always talking about food, too. These days people eat out a great deal more than they used to and, quite rightly, farm shops and farmers' markets are back in fashion.

We're taking ingredients seriously at last, but thankfully food is still a lot of fun. Of course, cooking can be hard work but there's nothing better than the thrill of taking something out of the oven and seeing it look just right. And making the dishes doesn't have to be difficult; the countless cookery programmes have familiarised us with all sorts of kitchen equipment, and these days more and more people are willing to have a go.

That's certainly the aim of this book – to make each recipe as easy to follow as possible, so that the dishes are a pleasure to make. Just remember that there's no rush and that cooking shouldn't be a chore. OK, so those teams of TV chefs create meals against the clock, but in my experience the joys of cooking come from just that – cooking – as well as eating the finished product, of course. And remember that you don't have to cook alone; our cookery classes are full of families and friends who come along to learn together.

So take your time. Read through each recipe before you begin, prepare your shopping list and see which dishes will complement one another well. Then get your ingredients ready in front of you, ascertain what equipment you'll need, and see what temperature the oven needs to be. Then simply take things step by step, and remember I'm with you every step of the way!

Richard Hughes

Tom Aikens was born in Norwich in 1970, grew up in Cringleford and attended Hethersett High. Along with his identical twin brother, Robert, Tom trained to be a chef at City College Norwich where his tutors included Richard Hughes. Tom completed a two-year Advanced Catering Diploma in 1989 and today has two highly-regarded London restaurants, the Michelin-starred Tom Aikens which opened to rave reviews in 2003; and the more informal, club-style restaurant, Tom's Kitchen, which opened in October 2006. Both restaurants are centrally located in Chelsea, just a stone's throw from the capital's fashionable King's Road. Tom Aikens married Amber Nuttall in June 2007. He still has friends and family in Norfolk and comes back to the county at least twice a year.

"When we were 16, my brother Rob and I applied to the Hotel School at City College Norwich. The interview didn't go very well and I think they only let me in because I was a twin; the Head of the Hotel School hated me! But being very determined, I thought, I'll show you! I believed in myself implicitly and I think I have showed them; I found something that I was good at, something that I loved. In the first year Rob and I were put together but in the second year they separated us because we used to misbehave. I definitely got something out of it, though, as we were lucky enough to have all the good teachers when I was there. I certainly remember being taught by Richard Hughes and he was great; it was a very good college and I really enjoyed it.

These days I go home about every six months or so. I've been to The Lavender House and I was very impressed. I went with Rob and Amber and my

other brother Mark and his wife and we enjoyed it. Norfolk is extremely lucky to have such fabulous produce. I remember when we were kids there used to be huge glasshouses near our home and we used to go and pick there in the summer: tomatoes, lettuces, cucumbers and celery, all sorts of salad items. We used to work all summer in those glasshouses and it was really hard work, 12 hour days from 6.30am to 6.30pm, but for young kids we were really raking it in!

These days I get some of the fish for my restaurants from Lowestoft; I get my cod from a boat there and all the fish is line-caught.

When we were kids we also used to go up to Blakeney, Holt and Holkham on the north Norfolk coast as well as to Orford in Suffolk.

My parents had a place in Blakeney – they still do – and we'd always go up there for holidays.

In fact, we still go there for holidays occasionally. Today, we're starting to see two types of chef. You see people who want to become a chef because they're passionate about food, and then you see the chefs who go into the profession for other purposes, seeing its potential. These days, the world of cooking is a lot calmer and more consistent in terms of the work and the hours, it's a different culture. But you still get people who are really driven and really focused. I still cook but I try to have a balance and I'm fortunate to have great people around me. I'm in the kitchen every day at Tom Aikens; every lunchtime and for every dinner. And I'd most definitely put myself in the category of chefs who are passionate about food. I've still got lots to learn – in fact, I'm learning every day – and I've got my goals of where I'm going next and what I've got to do. Every day we try to improve on what we've got at the restaurants and the food that we're producing. We hold a cooking course at Tom Aikens once a month; we take 14 people at a time and I cook five or six things: I go through the techniques then the guests get to eat every dish that I make. My stance since I started has changed hugely. Things are a lot simpler now. Over-elaborate food is too complicated, too fussy, too much, and, although it may look as if you've put a lot of effort and work into it, it's just too confusing. So every dish that I do now has no more than four ingredients; that's the food and the sauce.

If I went back to college now I would look at everything differently – it's very difficult to teach kids and it's very difficult to train someone from scratch. My time at the Hotel School at City College Norwich with Richard Hughes and the other tutors was really beneficial and worthwhile. When I come back to Norfolk, I rarely go out to eat because my Mum always wants to cook. But The Lavender House is definitely an exception!"

Tom Aikens, 43 Elystan Street, London, SW3 3NT
Tel: 020 7584 2003. Website: www.tomaikens.co.uk

Tom's Kitchen, 27 Cale Street, London, SW3 3QP
Tel: 020 7349 0202. Website: www.tomskitchen.co.uk

Awards and Accolades

Richard Hughes, The Lavender House and the team

2008

The Lavender House: The Good Food Guide	New Entry
The Lavender House: Michelin Guide	Recommended
The Lavender House: Square Meal	Recommended
The Lavender House: Harden's UK Restaurants	Recommended
The Lavender House: (From 2002 to date)	Two AA Rosettes
The Pigs pub in Edgefield:	Two AA Rosettes
Richard Knights: National Chef of the Year	Semi-Finalist
Julia Hetherton: National Young Chef of the Year	Semi-Finalist
Sam Matthews: National Young Waiter of the Year	Semi-Finalist
Jack Gosling and Jonathon Gay: EDP Norfolk Young Chef of the Future	Finalists
Laura Johnson: Hotel School Student of the Year (Restaurant Service)	Winner
The Lavender House: EDP Norfolk Restaurant of the Year	Finalist

2007

The Lavender House: Good Food Guide:	Recommended
The Lavender House: Michelin Guide:	Recommended
Richard Hughes: EDP Tourism Awards, Education & Training	Winner
Jamie Perry: Restaurant Association Young Waiter of the Year	Semi-Finalist

2006

Richard Hughes: UK TV Food Local Food Hero	Finalist
The Lavender House: Springboard Best UK Student Placement Provider	Winner
The Lavender House: Catey (Best Independent Marketing Campaign)	Winner
The Lavender House: EDP Tourism Awards, Innovation	Winner
Richard Hughes: EEDA BBC Work for Schools Premier Award	Winner
The Lavender House: EEDA BBC School/Business Link	Winner
Anna Simpson: BBC Outstanding Student of the Year	Winner
Julia Hetherton: EDP Norfolk Food Awards Young Chef of the Year	Winner
Julia Hetherton: Hoste Arms Norfolk Craft Student Competition	Winner
Richard Knights: National Chef of the Year	Semi-Finalist

2005

Richard Hughes: Norwich Hotel School Premier Award for Outstanding Contribution	Winner
Simon Hilburn: EDP Norfolk Food Awards Young Chef of the Future	Winner
Richard Hughes: EDP Norfolk Food Awards, Employment Innovation	Winner

2004

The Lavender House: Catey Menu of the Year	Winner
The Lavender House: EDP Norfolk Food Awards, Employment Innovation	Winner
Stacey Hughes: National Junior Master Chef	Runner-up

2003

The Lavender House: EDP Business Awards, Business/Education Link	Winner

Other

Richard Hughes: National Chef of the Year (1989, 1991, 1993)	Semi-Finalist
Richard Hughes: Baron Philippe de Rothschild Menu Competition (1988)	Runner-up

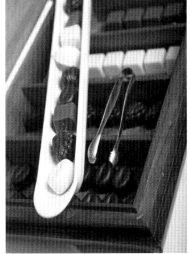  

Cutting the apron strings

It's a long time since I first started out on the road to becoming a chef. After writing to more than 40 hotels to try to get a job in the industry, I finally secured a place on the chefs' apprentice scheme at The Imperial Hotel in Great Yarmouth. One of my cousins had worked at the hotel before I started there and that stood me in good stead, but it took me ages to get used to being away from home, and moving to Yarmouth was a huge culture shock.

I started working at The Imperial Hotel at the tender age of 15, just three weeks before my 16th birthday and, having lived in the Fens all my life, I thought Great Yarmouth was the most exciting place on the planet! It was the late 1970s and it took us three hours to drive there from my parents' house in Christchurch in the Fens. To me, Great Yarmouth seemed like Las Vegas, with its glitzy fairground attractions, bars, restaurants and seafront hotels, and when I moved there I felt as if I was embarking on a massive adventure.

However, that was more than 30 years ago and I've worked in the hospitality business ever since. And I'm still thankful to Roger Mobbs, who owned The Imperial Hotel at the time, and the Head Chef Joe Gilham, for their training, their discipline and their endless patience. The apprenticeship scheme was a strict regime and only two school leavers were taken on every year; I spent two days a week washing up, two days a week in the kitchen, and one day a week at Great Yarmouth College to gain the necessary qualifications.

Fast forward almost 15 years and I opened my first restaurant, Number Twenty Four, in Wymondham. I'd always wanted to open my own place by the age of 30, and after hunting far and wide for suitable premises and borrowing against the house, I just made it. And so, with two small children in tow (our daughters Alison and Stacey were six and four at the time), we took over a small deli-cum-wine bar in the middle of Wymondham and worked round the clock cooking and cleaning and so on to make it work.

Looking back now, it seems like madness. But after working day and night, things started to look up and, best of all, the customers liked my cooking. My life as a chef has progressed from

there and things have gone from strength to strength. I'm not saying that we haven't had ups and downs – opening a second restaurant in Norwich city centre in 1994 was a terrible idea (we just weren't ready for two places then) and we closed it down shortly afterwards. But on the whole we've been lucky. Having sold Number Twenty Four in 2002, we took over The Old Beams in Brundall, changed the name to The Lavender House, and I've been there ever since.

If you've had dinner at The Lavender House, you'll know that this beautiful, thatched cottage is one of Norfolk's most historic buildings, dating back to 1540, and the attractive Robinia tree outside is one of the oldest of its kind in the country.

The building is fantastic and fortunately for me my staff are, too – my right-hand man Richard Knights, who these days does most of the cooking, is a real find, as are Julia Hetherton, Jonathon Gay, Jack Gosling, Sam Matthews, Maggie Crouch and all the rest of the team.

Before working for myself, I worked in all sorts of establishments, from the Michelin-starred Rookery Hall in Nantwich, Cheshire, to South Walsham Hall on the Norfolk Broads; I even had a secondment at The Ritz. Back in Norwich, I loved my job as Head Chef at the Theatre Royal during Dick Condon's reign, where we cooked for actors, performers and singers as well as for members of the audience.

These days I'm fortunate enough to have three fabulous restaurants; The Lavender House in Brundall, The Pigs pub in Edgefield, and the Anna Sewell House Restaurant in Great Yarmouth. And I'm pleased to say that more than 30 years after starting out, I still love my job as a chef.

Why did you decide to publish this book?

We want people to be able to replicate what we teach during the cookery classes at The Lavender House, as well as the recipes that we publish in newspapers and magazines. Often chefs show things that nobody is ever going to attempt at home but they're not encouraging people to cook like that – if you create something that's incredibly difficult using ingredients that people can't get, it'll just put people off. So I'm hoping that this book will actually make people want to cook the dishes.

How did you choose the dishes?

There's a big cross section. Some would stand up in the restaurant at The Lavender House, some are far more homely, more the sort of thing that you'd cook for your tea at home. They're all pretty straightforward; there are no ingredients that are difficult to get hold of, and a lot use local produce.

Are there any dishes you particularly like?

A lot of the fish ones have come out really well, and yet they're probably the simplest things to cook; fish can be very easy. There are also lots of barbecue dishes and desserts – desserts are one of our really strong points.

Do you have a signature dish?

Well, a while ago The Lavender House was selected as one of The Times' top 10 most romantic restaurants in the country, and they picked out the peanut butter parfait which was great, that's certainly one of our most popular desserts. And, of course, we always have beef on our menu from our great friend David Barnard who farms, butchers and sells down in Shropham. I've used David's beef, lamb and pork since I had my first restaurant in Wymondham, and I've always had consistently great compliments about the meat. In cookery there is a saying: "The better you buy, the less you have to do to it," and that's certainly true.

What sort of training did you have?

As I mentioned on the previous pages, I was one of the chefs taken on to participate in the apprenticeship scheme run by The Imperial Hotel in Great Yarmouth. At The Lavender House we have just launched the Professional Chefs' Apprenticeship Scheme so we can give proper, thorough training in our own kitchens, so things have come full circle. There's no substitute for day-to-day graft in a real working environment, and I would recommend taking the apprenticeship route rather than attending college full time.

What does your job involve?

Well, I'm at The Lavender House every day; I very rarely miss a shift. Things have changed quite dramatically over the past two years or so, though, as Richard Knights does most of the

cooking now, and I'm the link between the kitchen and the restaurant. We work on the new menus together and I run the cookery school-side of things which is a big part of the business. I'll usually take three classes a week, normally one on a Tuesday night, probably a "Chef For A Day" during the week and another one on Saturday morning. I also cover the restaurant shifts, and if Richard's not there, I'll cover for him. Richard runs the nuts and bolts of the restaurant service and I handle all the extras: the cookery school, publicity events, cookery demonstrations and marketing the business. There's also an incredible amount of paperwork.

What sort of cookery classes do you offer?

We do all sorts, lots of demos and loads of hands-on work where people can come in and actually cook. We run the cookery experience called "Chef For A Day", hold corporate days for local businesses, and we take lots of work experience people. They're mainly from schools, and most of them are around 15. If you get the right ones, it can work out very well – four of our current staff came to us that way.

And you hold cookery classes for children?

Yes, we invite a class into the restaurant every month and they have a tour of the kitchen and then lunch. We don't give them the run-of-the-mill things, it's always something very different, and then they have a cookery demonstration. We've had visits from so many schools, from four-year-olds to 18-year-olds. Not only do we teach them about food and how to eat well, but they also get to enjoy one another's company in a formal restaurant setting. Most importantly, though, we show them that the crucial thing in life is to enjoy your work. So many people have the attitude that their job is just a means to earn funds so they can enjoy themselves but we believe that you can have your cake and eat it.

How do you divide your time?

I go over to The Pigs once a week. When it first opened I was cooking there almost on a daily basis and it was hard work – it was like stepping back in time to when I opened my first restaurant, Number Twenty Four in Wymondham. Nowadays, however, things are much more settled at The Pigs and we've got a new kitchen and a really strong team. I cook there when the chefs are on holiday and I love it because it's fast and furious. The food there is much simpler than it is at The Lavender House and the atmosphere is more relaxed. As with everything in this trade, it's all about getting the right people, and when you find them you've got to keep hold of them. The Manager, Cloe Wasey, who was there from the beginning, and the Head Chef Tim Abbott, now have a stake in the business and they care about it as much as I do.

As for the Anna Sewell House Restaurant in Yarmouth, we set that up in the autumn of 2007 and things are much simpler there. There's a relaxed atmosphere and we use a lot of organic food and change the menu every single day. It's what's called a "market garden kitchen" as Julia Hetherton, our Head Chef, looks at the produce available each day and then changes the menu according to what's on offer. This approach seems to be going down well.

Do you cater for people with special diets?

Yes, it's no problem at all, they're a big part of our business. Many chefs complain about that side of things but for us it's a big plus and we do a huge amount of trade because we offer exciting vegetarian food as well as food for celiacs, diabetics, those on low-cholesterol diets and so on. We try to approach things with the right attitude and to give people an experience that they're not going to get anywhere else.

Do you listen to music when you cook?

No, not now. I did when I worked on my own but nowadays we don't, simply because we've all got different tastes and I don't want to impose my taste on others. We always have the football on on a Saturday afternoon, though, without fail. Everybody supports Norwich except me - I'm a West Ham supporter. People ask me why I support West Ham but when I was a

boy I lived in the middle of the Fens, and Norwich could have been on the other side of the moon for all I knew! My Mum used to love Bobby Moore, so that's how it all started. But they're all Norwich fans in the restaurant, so that's good fun. I still like to go to see West Ham; I used to go quite a bit on Sunday nights and Mondays, and I like to go to see Norwich with the guys from the kitchen. I think there is much to be admired about the way Norwich City is run. Fans are always going to complain, but I think Norwich City is a great example of how to run a business.

Do you work long hours?

On most days I'm in the restaurant by 9am and I don't get away until midnight. On Saturday mornings I'm in earlier because we have a cookery class, so I get in at 8am, although I do try to have a bit of a break in the afternoon on Saturdays because we'll work until about 1am. On Sundays we normally start at 10am and we're out by about 4pm. I try to have Mondays off but there's always something going on - I pop in for 10 minutes and I'm there half the day!

What do you eat when you're at work?

Well, we used to eat together but the trouble is that as soon as we're under pressure that's something that falls by the wayside. So I just eat loads of Julia's chocolates which isn't the done thing. I eat a fair amount at the

restaurant in order to try things, but I've got a really sweet tooth and no doubt that will be my downfall. I love children's sweets, chocolate and ice cream, and that's partly why desserts are such a strong part of our offer; they're really strong in terms of the flavours and what they look like.

Do you cook for your friends and family?

Very rarely, simply because I only spend about one morning a week at home. Cooking at home can be rather frustrating. I'm an instinctive cook; I'll just look to see what we've got and go from there, but I find I never have everything I need at home.

Which chefs do you admire?

I admire a lot of the great French chefs, because they've been cooking all their lives, people such as Paul Bocuse who has been cooking since he was 14. In this country, people such as the Roux brothers who went into the industry when they were very young and are still at it years and years later. Also because they were so instrumental in setting people on their way – nowadays it's very fashionable for children to say that they want to be chefs, but the Roux brothers encouraged others at a time when cooking wasn't quite so in vogue. I admire people who have a great grounding in cooking – Bryan Turner, for example, and Tom Aikens, of course, because he's a local lad. Tom isn't very

old, but he's had a strong career path and has always known what he wants to do. I also admire Gordon Ramsay – he's a massive TV personality, but he has the substance to back himself up.

I think celebrity chefs are absolutely fine if they've been through the mill of the kitchen and have that kind of background behind them – at least 10 or 15 years of solid work. Gary Rhodes is also really inspirational, because he was one of the first people to get into modern British cooking. I've met him two or three times and he's very constructive, he's somebody who understands food, and has opened up lots of restaurants. He's known for his silly haircut but he's been cooking since he was 16 and he knows the pressure and how the business works.

However, there are an awful lot of chefs who are just as talented and just as dedicated as the big names but many of them simply get on with the job quietly without seeking the fame – they just love to cook.

On a business level, I admire my partner at The Pigs pub, Iain Wilson, of Byfords' fame (Byfords Café, Deli and Posh B&B in Holt); he's a real inspiration. He's a complete one-off who never fails to motivate people to achieve their goals. Partnerships are notorious for being tricky, particularly when you've been used to doing your own thing, but we've been working

together for over two years now and, though we've had many frank discussions, we've never fallen out. I've learnt loads from him, which shows you can teach an old dog new tricks.

Do you follow any of the cookery shows?

Yes, I watch some of them. I love the re-runs of Keith Floyd, I still find them really funny. And there's a series on Sky with Anthony Bourdain going round the world looking at different cultures and trying out their food and that's quite interesting. He's a funny guy and a good presenter. I don't like the more flippant ones, as they haven't got anything to do with cooking – all this trying to cook a meal in 20 minutes or so isn't helpful because most of the time you have to spend longer than 20 minutes to get a result. After all, other than stir-fries, there's not a lot you can do in 20 minutes, is there?

Do you have a favourite cookery book?

Floyd in the Soup is a potted history, cartoon-type book of Keith Floyd when he started out, and that's a great book, and Nico Ladenis brought out a book in the 1980s called My Gastronomy which was really inspirational at the time. Not only did it feature recipes but also his philosophy about the restaurants. And I love Nose to Tail Eating by Fergus Henderson at St John in Smithfield, that's a great book because it's about getting back to the ingredients. The

young chefs buy all the coffee table books such as the Gordon Ramsay ones, and they're fine, but the Jane Grigson and Elizabeth David books will stand the test of time.

How do you feel about restaurant critics?

I'd love more of them to come to The Lavender House to see what they think! Basically, restaurant critics are there for the customer and it's all about entertainment. If you've got a regular customer base and you're well established, it's a bit of fun really. But I read the reviews and I think they're really interesting – I like them when they actually say something, I hate those wishy-washy ones.

What's the best meal you've ever eaten?

Great meals depend on where you are, who you're with and the situation. The grandest meal I ever had was in a place called Le Moulin de Lourmarin in Provence. I was inspired by this restaurant as a great friend has an apartment in the village and she would often bring me back brochures and menus. It was a real highlight when I finally got to eat there in the spring of 2007. And I took all the staff from The Lavender House to Gordon Ramsay's place on Hospital Road in London and that was absolutely stunning.

When I was 21, I went to Le Soufflé at the Hotel InterContinental London

and that sticks in my mind as it was one of the first really grand meals I'd ever had – at 21 I'd never seen anything like that before. But as I said, a fantastic meal doesn't have to be grand – it can be fish and chips on the seafront if the weather and company are right.

Have you had any particularly bad meals?

Well, for a long time, British pub food was horrendous, and some of the meals in the mid-1980s, when the mid-range pubs were getting microwaves and into the ready-meal market, were just appallingly bad! Thankfully, though, most of them have fallen by the wayside now.

How do you come up with your menus?

At The Lavender House we change the menu every month without fail. One or two dishes stay the same; there's always Barnard's beef on there, for example, and the fish changes more often because it depends on what our fish supplier, Gary Howard, has got.

Richard Knights and I work on the menus together, and we always plan them around what's available. Some chefs will write the menu and then try to source the food but we always find out what's on the market and what's good and then go from there.

Where does your produce come from?

A lot of it comes from local farm shops such as the HFG Farm Shops,

they're a great source of inspiration as well as a source of ingredients. We use David Barnard in Attleborough for our meat because we've known him for a long time and we know his operation back to front, and the Barnards are really nice people to deal with. We don't have masses of suppliers to be honest. Norwich has a lot of great independent food stores and also great places for cookware such as Jarrolds and Looses Cookshop – they're Norfolk institutions and one of the things that makes Norwich such an attractive place.

How many diners can you accommodate?

When we're absolutely full, we can take 48 in the restaurant and eight sitting on the kitchen table, but that's full!

Can you tell us about the kitchen table?

The chef's table is a relatively new thing for us. We built it at the end of 2007 and it's the only one of its sort in the county. It seats up to eight people and it's incredibly popular. It's literally next door to the kitchen and it's open-plan, so that the customers can see everything that goes on. It's air-conditioned so it's nice and cool, and it offers a ringside seat of the chefs in action. People have been so enthusiastic about it – they absolutely love sitting there. They love seeing the chefs working hard and they see such a range of dishes being made – there's always great excitement when they see

their food coming out. And as the night wears on and we start to relax a little, we'll often get customers up to cook their own dishes – we even had one guy clearing up at the end of the night and his friends were taking pictures of him sweeping and mopping the floor!

The kitchen table has been a massive success for us, and we have customers eating there nearly every Friday and Saturday night. People just love to see what goes on in kitchens these days.

Have you had any funny moments?

Yes, where should I start?! Years ago, when we used to do a lot of outside catering, we had numerous mishaps. Once, at a very grand country house in South Norfolk, a stray Labrador ate the bottom tier of a wedding cake before the bride and groom arrived. We've also had some major disasters. Recently we had some problems with the electrics at the Anna Sewell House Restaurant in Yarmouth (they're fixed now, thank goodness) and all the lights went out at 8 o'clock; and we had the the same thing at The Lavender House when we first bought it. I don't know why, but I seem to be cursed with electrics!

Another time we took on a large outside catering function – a barbecue for 200 people at night – and the people we were working for didn't remember the lights so we had to barbecue all the food in the dark. People often say to me that

I couldn't make it up and that's one of the things that inspired me to collate the stories in my first book, Hughes Cooking? The rants, reflections and recipes of Richard Hughes.

What keeps you motivated?

The thing that motivates me most are the people I work with as they care about cooking just as much as I do. When you have a 15-year-old boy working with you and you can see how much he loves his work, it's incredibly motivating.

Do you have any advice for would-be chefs?

The trick is to get work experience in any form, even washing up, just so you can see the environment you're going into. And remember that cooking and running a restaurant are completely divorced – they've got nothing to do with each other.

Where do you think the industry is heading?

Well, food is a lot simpler now, and it's gone back to its roots; you've only got to look at our pub, The Pigs in Edgefield, to see how well it's doing by serving real classics. As people cook less at home, there's a real market for home cooking in pubs and restaurants, perhaps because people eat out all the time now. Many people want to know where their food comes from, who's produced it and so on. The business needs to be honest and accept and embrace the new level of transparency required.

Has cooking changed since you started?

It's almost come full circle. When I started out, cooking was based around the French traditions and culture, then it became very trendy and Nouvelle Cuisine came in. Food can be a lot simpler these days, though I'm not sure how much the healthy eating campaign actually affects people's eating habits when they're eating out for pleasure. However, diners are more willing to accept something that's simply prepared as long as the ingredients are top-notch.

Do you still enjoy your job?

I enjoy it more now than I ever have done, I really do. I'm working with the right people, and also customers understand the food more now than they used to, they understand how it all works. And I love The Lavender House – the actual building – it's a thrill working there every day.

How do you relax outside the kitchen?

I sleep! As I said, I'm a big football fan and I watch the football when it's on. I've got a huge CD collection and I used to go to quite a lot of gigs with my eldest daughter, Alison. We've also managed to go to a couple of festivals which were a real hoot. I like a range of music; seeing Morrissey at Camden Roundhouse was a big highlight, and we used to go to the UEA quite a lot. And when I first started in Yarmouth, we used to hitchhike to West Runton,

that's a long hitchhike! They used to have bands at the little pavilion on the seafront – I saw The Clash, The Buzzcocks, the UK Subs... all the big names have played there. For people of my age it holds a lot of fond memories.

I also love to read; I always have two or three books on the go at once, covering a range of subjects from political biographies to modern wars. I have to read for at least 30 minutes to wind down at the end of a busy night.

Do you eat out very much?

Absolutely. Eating out is a pleasure and a job, and I usually go down to London once every six weeks or so, often taking my youngest daughter, Stacey, who's something of a restaurant critic!

Have you cooked for anyone famous?

Quite a few footballers and a number of well-known chefs including Tom Aikens, Bryan Turner and Rick Stein. When we had Number Twenty Four, Chelsea came in – Glenn Hoddle and Ken Bates. Ken Bates was still there at 20 to three!

Do you have any further ambitions?

My big ambition is to write a novel. And I'd love to tour France, visiting all the great restaurants and vineyards.

Whom would you most like to cook for?

Anyone who appreciates good food, but I'd rather someone cooked for me!

The Lavender House

A celebrated restaurant, chefs' training centre and bustling cookery school.

Those of you who are already familiar with The Lavender House in Brundall will know just what a lovely building it is. This charming thatched property dates back to the 16th century and its low ceiling, many beams and narrow corridors help create the enchanting atmosphere that has made so many meals and celebrations a success. This Grade II-listed cottage in the heart of the village has been home to The Lavender House Restaurant & Cookery School since we bought the building back in 2002. Today it not only houses a busy restaurant and chefs' training kitchen but also a popular and very active cookery school.

Fortunately we have built up quite a following and our style of cookery, which we like to call "Modern Norfolk" has brought us a number of accolades. The restaurant has been featured on television many times, including on the BBC's Rick Stein Food Heroes, UK Sky Food and ITV's Flying Picnic, and has been included in local and national newspapers as well as all sorts of guidebooks. In addition, I contribute regularly to the Eastern Daily Press and EDP Norfolk magazine, something I really enjoy, and we receive many requests for recipes from our customers. Thanks to my skilled team of chefs and welcoming front of house staff, The Lavender House continues to prove popular with all sorts of customers, from those enjoying an intimate meal for two, to those celebrating a birthday, anniversary or even a wedding breakfast.

These days, the cookery school side of the business is just as busy as the restaurant, and we take three to four cookery classes a week. Sometimes we work with individuals hoping to improve their culinary skills or who wish to impress their friends; sometimes it's with a group of budding cooks learning how to cook with fish, meat or chocolate, for example. There are even classes for teams of work colleagues keen to glean as much as they can from the kitchen on a team building day. All sorts of cookery events are on offer, from cheese tasting, fast food and desserts, to food for barbecues, perfect pastries, and sessions on beer tasting and food pairing.

Like all those passionate about food, we use fresh, local, seasonal ingredients. We try to be innovative with flavours and inventive with presentation, and we hope that it's this combination that keeps our customers coming back for more and recommending others to us.

As we say in our brochure: "Don't expect the intimidating cathedral-like atmosphere that so many top restaurants seem to radiate: we are looking to have fun. Whether you're at The Lavender House for a romantic occasion, a family celebration or a corporate dinner, we believe our passion for our craft will ensure that the event is a success." It's all about enjoying yourselves.

The Lavender House, 39 The Street, Brundall, Norfolk, NR13 5AA. Tel: 01603 712215.
Website: www.thelavenderhouse.co.uk

Situated in the heart of the Norfolk Broads just 10 minutes from Norwich city centre, The Lavender House is open for dinner from Wednesday to Saturday and for Sunday lunch.

The Pigs
Oink if you prefer a proper pub!

The Pigs pub in Edgefield has had various guises. This popular place was previously known as 'The Three Pigs' but when we bought it we changed the name to 'The Pigs' as that's what all the locals called it. This fabulous pub, located on the Norwich Road three miles south of Holt, is a joint venture between Richard Hughes Restaurants Ltd and Iain Wilson of Byfords of Holt, the well-known Café, Deli and Posh B&B (www.byfords.org.uk).

Purchased in October 2006, The Pigs has undergone a nose-to-tail makeover and now boasts a fabulous bar, conservatory-style restaurant, family room, children's play area and a big garden. But the best thing about The Pigs – besides the friendly staff, of course – is the food. Naturally, you can get a great pint at the bar or contemplate life over a glass or two of wine, but if you're a fan of proper pub grub, you'll love the menu at The Pigs.

Head Chef Tim Abbott and his team have put together a marvellous menu featuring local, seasonal food – game from the Edgefield shoots, mutton from Salhouse, pork from Swannington, lamb from Shropham, crabs from Cromer, mussels from Brancaster, herrings from Caister, and fruit and veg fresh from the farm shops. Plus there's a host of local ales, with beer from Woodbastwick, Holt and even across the border in Southwold.

Pig In Control is the lovely Cloe Wasey and she and the rest of the team will be happy to welcome you whether you're visiting for a quick bite on your way to the beach or treating yourself to a leisurely three-course meal. For those who are peckish, there are all sorts of treats on offer, from beef dripping on toast with sea salt; Norfolk rabbit made with Woodforde's Wherry, Norfolk Dapple, Colman's mustard, thickly-cut bread and apple chutney; to potted ham hock with home-made piccalilli and Cley smoked shell-on prawns. And if you're feeling a little hungrier, there's The Pigs' popular plate of piggy pieces: sausage, black pudding, bacon, ham, pigs' ears, crackling and pork cheese.

More substantial main courses include The Three Pigs, the pub's signature dish, consisting of slow-cooked belly of pork, smoky bacon beans, black pudding and apple chutney; rosemary roasted free-range chicken; pan-fried lamb's liver; an 8oz rump steak; and traditional fisherman's pie. Plus there's a specials board featuring all sorts of seasonal dishes.

These are very tasty but there's something even better to come – the delightful desserts which include Aspalls cider jelly; dark chocolate truffle with Baileys syllabub; lavender and lemon posset; strawberry fool; the local artisans' cheeseboard and the sumptuous sticky brick pudding. And if you're a real dessert fan, you'll love the Sunday Pudding Club where you can visit the pudding table as often as you wish.

The Pigs pub is anything but pretentious; come and visit us for a quick half, join in the Wednesday quiz, treat yourself to a leisurely meal, or simply sun yourself all day in the garden. And if you grow any fruit or veg or join in the local shoots, then show us what you've got to offer and we may be able to do a deal!

The Pigs, Norwich Road, Edgefield, Holt, NR24 2RL
Tel: 01263 587634. Website: www.thepigs.org.uk

Open from 11am to 3pm and 6pm to 11pm, Tuesday to Saturday; and from noon to 4pm (food until 3pm) on Sundays and Bank Holidays.

The Anna Sewell House Restaurant

Probably the most romantic restaurant in the country!

If you haven't yet visited our restaurant in Great Yarmouth, then you're in for a real treat. Built in 1620, Anna Sewell House is one of the most interesting buildings in Norfolk – it was the birthplace of Anna Sewell, who wrote the children's favourite, Black Beauty, and this delightful cottage was a museum until the late 1970s. After being threatened with demolition, it was given listed status and in the last few decades it has been home to a press agency, offices and a tearoom. In October 2007 the building was acquired by Richard Hughes Restaurants Ltd, and since then this charming place has been home to the Anna Sewell House Restaurant and is now a showcase for Head Chef Julia Hetherton's wonderful cooking.

Behind the doll's house façade of this intriguing building a fascinating food revolution is taking place. Diners are treated to a market kitchen-style menu, with the dishes changing on a daily basis according to the produce available. As always, the finest, freshest ingredients are used, with the dishes inspired by the market on the day.

Julia's culinary idols include Elizabeth David, Jane Grigson, and Alice Waters of Chez Panisse in California, and she cooks with a genuine love of food. As Alice Waters says: "Eating is a political act, from the family to the school, the neighbourhood, the nation, the world, you can take part in a delicious revolution."

The Anna Sewell House Restaurant is a cosy, neighbourhood restaurant that aims to be at the heart of the community, and the food presented is perfect for get-togethers with family and friends. The restaurant is also available for hire for parties of between 12 and 16.

Before taking over the helm at Anna Sewell House, Julia worked at The Lavender House for several years. She has won several awards for her cooking and has enjoyed work experience with Raymond Blanc at Le Manoir aux Quat Saisons in Oxfordshire, and with top chef Angela Hartnett at The Connaught in London.

Julia was born at the James Paget Hospital in Gorleston but spent her youth in Zimbabwe before returning to East Anglia to study at the Hotel School at City College Norwich.

So what can you expect at the Anna Sewell House Restaurant? Well, it's small but perfectly formed, seating a maximum of 20 diners and with a first floor bar reached by a narrow staircase, where you can enjoy an aperitif or coffee. In addition to the daily menu, there's an interesting wine list featuring unusual bottles at reasonable prices sourced by Eastern Daily Press columnist Keith Reeves of Weavers Way Wine. This lovely place is perfect for a romantic dinner for two or a special occasion, but is just as suitable for a quick one-course lunch with a glass of wine on a working weekday. For a sample menu, please just visit the restaurant's website at: www.annasewellhouserestaurant.co.uk

The Anna Sewell House Restaurant is at
26 Church Plain, Great Yarmouth, NR30 1NE
Website: www.annasewellhouserestaurant.co.uk
Tel: 01493 856859. Open for lunch from noon on Wednesday, Thursday and Friday, and for dinner from 6pm on Thursday and Friday. A special five course menu is available on Saturday evenings.
Dining is by reservation only, and a free car park is located on Church Plain.

Contents

Desserts

Sweet things

Starters

As every good cook knows, a starter can make or break a meal. You need to think about the other dishes you're going to serve later and ensure that the textures and tastes complement one another well. As always, it's also a good idea to use produce that's in season and which goes with the weather on the day; ice-cold gazpacho will go down best on a gloriously sunny day while the spiced parsnip and coconut soup is best served in the winter months.

Of course, you can always pad these out with some fresh bread and salad for a light lunch or midweek supper.

I was just 15 when I first visited a real hotel, the Imperial Hotel in Great Yarmouth, on the day I had my interview for my first proper job. Proving that good food never goes out of fashion, I'm still using recipes from my time there and this one is one of the best.

Ingredients

Serves four (freezable)

4 kipper fillets
250g cream cheese
Squeeze lemon juice
Squeeze lime juice
1 dessertspoon tomato ketchup
1 ripe tomato
2 sticks celery
1 teaspoon curry powder
Small bunch flat-leaf parsley, roughly chopped
½ cucumber, peeled
Salt and freshly ground black pepper
1 dessertspoon chopped chives
Few slices interesting bread

Step by step

1. Poach the kipper fillets in a little boiling water for around five minutes.

2. Meanwhile, dice the celery, tomatoes and cucumber.

3. Remove the fish from the water, take off the skin with a knife then flake the flesh away from the bones.

4. Place the fish in a food processor and blend.

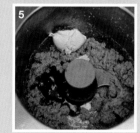

5. Add the cream cheese and the ketchup.

6. Stir in the lemon and lime juice.

7. Add the cucumber mixture, curry powder and parsley then blend again.

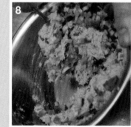

8. Mix thoroughly then season well with salt and pepper.

9. Pile the paste into attractive, individual little pots.

10. Garnish with chives and serve with slices of bread or toast.

This is a fantastic dish for a picnic or late summer lunch and can even be eaten for breakfast.

When it comes to special occasions, such as a wedding anniversary or an important birthday, for example, it can be difficult to think of dishes that will keep everybody happy. Often the simplest, tried-and-tested ones work best, so what could be better than a prawn cocktail?

Ingredients

Serves four

250g best quality prawns
8 small new potatoes, cooked
25g red onion
2 small sticks celery and tops
2 dessertspoons crème fraîche
Large bunch flat-leaf parsley
1 large, ripe avocado
2 dessertspoons extra virgin olive oil
Juice of 1 lemon
Large pinch mild curry spice
2 tomatoes, peeled
1 small cucumber, with some peel removed
Salt and freshly milled black pepper

Step by step

1 Finely dice the new potatoes, the celery and the red onion.

2 Place these in a bowl, add the crème fraîche and season with salt and pepper. Mix well then set them aside.

3 Scoop the flesh from the avocados.

4 Mix this with half the lemon juice, the curry spice and the olive oil. Mash together then set aside.

5 Season the prawns with salt and pepper and the remaining lemon juice. Chop the tomatoes and parsley and mix this in.

6 Assemble the cocktails: Slice the cucumber then arrange this decoratively on the plates.

7 Place a pastry cutter in the middle of the cucumber slices and press the potato salad into the base.

8 Add a layer of the avocado mixture, almost to the top.

9 Pile the prawns carefully on top.

10 Remove the ring gently, garnish with a celery leaf and serve immediately.

To bring this dish bang-up-to-date, you can substitute the prawns for peeled brown shrimps.

Once you've mastered this basic soup recipe you will have increased your culinary repertoire considerably. That's because you can substitute the parsnips for all sorts of other ingredients such as celery and apple, sweet potato or even beetroot with vodka and black pepper.

Ingredients

Serves four (freezable)

500g parsnips
1 x 400ml can coconut milk
1 teaspoon curry powder
1 litre vegetable stock
1 large onion
50g butter
4 teaspoons sour cream
4 teaspoons chopped coriander
Salt and white pepper

Step by step

Finely dice the onion.

Add the curry powder then fry until soft.

Peel, core and chop the parsnips.

Place in a saucepan with the coconut milk.

Slowly add the vegetable stock.

Heat the liquid and leave to simmer.

When the parsnips are soft (around 25 minutes) blend until smooth. Season with salt and white pepper.

Pass the liquid through a strainer.

Ladle into warm bowls.

Place a spoonful of sour cream on top and decorate with some chopped coriander.

If you make more than you need and freeze the rest, you'll always have a tasty snack to hand.

There'll only be a handful of summer days when you can enjoy a cold soup properly. They need to be absolutely sweltering as then the zing of the iced, ripe vegetables will bring an unexpected thrill to alfresco dining. This dish is best enjoyed when sitting outside in the heat of the sun.

Ingredients

Makes four generous portions (freezable)

6 large, ripe tomatoes
2 red peppers
1 onion
4 spring onions
1 cucumber
2 cloves garlic
Large bunch fresh herbs: rosemary, parsley, basil, fennel and celery leaf
1 lime
1 glass dry white wine
125ml extra virgin olive oil
25ml white wine vinegar
325ml iced water
Rock salt and black pepper

Step by step

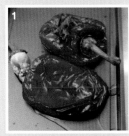

1 Place the red peppers on a baking tray and roast them in the oven for 15 minutes at 200C/ Gas Mark 6.

2 Skin and de-seed the roasted peppers then return them to the tray.

3 Finely chop the onion, the tomatoes and the garlic then add these to the peppers.

4 Add the olive oil, rosemary, salt and pepper then roast again for 15 minutes.

5 When cooked, blend the vegetables until smooth. Add the wine and some iced water before blending again.

6 Add some olive oil and the white wine vinegar and then whiz the mixture up again.

7 Do the same thing with the fresh herbs.

8 Pass the mixture through a fine strainer.

9 Add the lime juice then adjust with iced water (it needs to be really cold). Season liberally.

10 Place in bowls and decorate with chopped spring onion and tomato and a drizzle of olive oil.

To make this extra special, pile a little fresh Cromer crab into each bowl and serve with slices of toast.

This is a great dish for a celebration; simply make daintier blinis and serve them as canapés. Traditionally they're served with smoked salmon but you can use cream cheese with slices of cucumber or tomato. If you're feeling extravagant, you can top them with sour cream and caviar.

Ingredients

Makes 12 to 16 (freezable)

For the ferment
25g plain flour
15g fresh yeast
50ml milk
Pinch sugar

For the batter
125g flour
150ml milk
Two eggs, separated
Good pinch salt
1 dessertspoon parsley, chives and thyme
1 dessertspoon olive oil
10g butter

For the topping
4 slices smoked salmon
100ml whipping cream
Juice of ½ lemon
1 teaspoon creamed horseradish

Step by step

Make the ferment: Warm the milk, crumble in the yeast and add the sugar then stir to dissolve.

Add the flour to the yeast mixture and whisk lightly.

Cover the bowl with a cloth and keep warm for five minutes or so until the yeast begins to bubble.

Make the batter: Place the flour and salt in a bowl and add the chopped herbs.

Add the egg yolks to the flour mixture followed by the milk then whisk thoroughly.

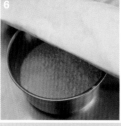

Stir in the ferment, cover again and leave in a warm place until double in volume (around 10 minutes).

Whisk the egg whites until stiff then fold them into the risen mixture.

Heat the oil and butter. When smoking slightly, add spoonfuls of the batter and fry for three minutes on each side.

Make the horseradish cream: Whip the cream lightly with a squeeze of lemon juice then add the horseradish.

Place the blinis on a plate with the salmon and horseradish cream. Serve while the blinis are still warm.

For a special occasion you can make the blinis in advance as they freeze really well.

This is a lovely-looking dish and the smell of it cooking is bound to get those taste buds going. It works well as a starter, but if you feel like something more substantial you can turn it into a main course by supplementing it with some rice or a bowl of couscous.

Ingredients

Serves four

20 peeled prawn tails
1 clove garlic
1 large piece ginger
Large piece red, yellow and green pepper
1 glass dry white wine
2 dessertspoons whipping or double cream
1 large courgette
125g butter
Few leaves fresh basil

Step by step

Finely chop the ginger and garlic.

Melt the butter in a saucepan and add the prawn tails.

Add the garlic and ginger then fry for two to three minutes.

Dice the peppers.

Add the diced peppers to the prawns.

Add the cream and the white wine.

Shred the basil leaves.

Peel, slice and dice the courgette.

Add the butter to the prawn mixture.

Place the diced courgette and basil in the mixture then spoon into shallow dishes and garnish with basil.

This is a really quick dish to prepare and a favourite from our fast food cookery demonstrations.

This dish differs from traditional onion tart as shallots are slightly stronger. If you want to ring the changes further still try adding some chopped apple or, at Christmas time, some chestnuts. A heavy-bottomed frying pan that goes straight in the oven works best for this.

Ingredients

Serves four

750g shallots
125g ready-made puff pastry
2 dessertspoons balsamic vinegar
25g granulated sugar
50g butter

Step by step

1 Simmer the onions in a pan of boiling water for five minutes.

2 Take the onions out of the water and peel.

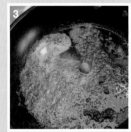

3 Heat the butter and sugar together in a heavy frying pan.

4 Add the onions and fry until nicely coloured.

5 Add the vinegar and continue to fry, reducing to a glaze.

6 Roll the puff pastry out on a floured surface.

7 Using a plate, cut out a large round of pastry, enough to fill the pan.

8 Press the pastry down gently over the onions in the pan.

9 Place in the oven at 190C/Gas Mark 5 until golden (around 15 minutes).

10 Turn out carefully.

It's best to leave the skin on the onions when you simmer them as this will make them easier to peel.

This dish works well with any strong cheese so if you're not a fan of Stilton you can substitute it with Binham Blue, Roquefort or even goat's cheese if you prefer. As the soufflé is hot and rich, it makes a wonderful winter starter and is perfect in the run-up to Christmas.

Ingredients

Serves four (freezable)

200g Stilton
300ml milk
1 onion
2 eggs
50g plain flour
50g butter
Pinch paprika
Freshly milled black pepper
Pinch salt

Step by step

1 Slice the onion, add the milk and paprika and bring to the boil then simmer for 15 minutes and strain.

2 Melt the butter, add the flour and cook for three minutes, stirring continuously.

3 Slowly add the boiled milk, stirring continuously.

4 Beat well to form a smooth, thick sauce then mix in three quarters of the Stilton.

5 Place the sauce in a clean bowl and beat in the egg yolks then leave to cool.

6 Whisk the egg whites with a tiny pinch of salt.

7 Fold the whisked egg whites gently into the cool sauce.

8 Butter and flour the ramekins then divide the mixture between them.

9 Place in a roasting tin with boiling water halfway up their sides. Bake at 180C/Gas Mark 4 for 15 minutes. Cool.

10 Put on an ovenproof dish. Top with the cream and Stilton. Bake at 200C/Gas Mark 6 until golden (six minutes).

These soufflés freeze well; bake them once then freeze them until needed and bake them again.

These savoury trifles look fantastic when served in individual glasses, such as the Martini glasses I've used here. With the pear chutney as a base, followed by layers of walnuts, cheese and red pepper relish, they resemble sweet trifles and always prove to be a conversation piece.

Ingredients

Makes four

400g Binham Blue cheese
2 ripe pears
1 dessertspoon walnuts
½ red pepper
½ small onion
2 dessertspoons whipping or double cream
1 teaspoon white wine vinegar
1 teaspoon sugar
Small bunch flat-leaf parsley

Step by step

1

Make the pear chutney: Peel, core and dice the pears and place them in a pan.

2

Finely dice a dessertspoon of onion and add this to the pears then soften them in a little butter.

3

Add the sugar and vinegar to the pear mixture.

4

Crush the walnuts in a bowl then chop and add the parsley.

5

Slice the pepper and the remaining onion then fry until soft.

6

Soften the cheese with a wooden spoon.

7

Place a layer of the onion mixture in a glass.

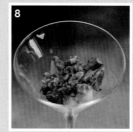

8

Add a layer of walnuts and parsley.

9

Pipe or spoon the blue cheese mixture on top.

10

Garnish with the red pepper and onion mix.

If you can't find Binham Blue you can use any other soft blue cheese instead, or even goat's cheese.

This salad includes some fabulous slow-roasted tomatoes. Drying them out in the oven accentuates their sweetness so that they rival those lovely sun-dried ones from the South of France. If you're a keen gardener, adapt this to use whatever vegetables you have available.

Ingredients

Serves four

600g assorted summer vegetables (peppers, aubergine, courgette, asparagus)

100g mozzarella

200g ripe tomatoes

1 lemon

Bunch fresh basil

Bunch fresh parsley

8 dessertspoons light olive oil

2 teaspoons freshly chopped garlic

2 dessertspoons balsamic vinegar

Salt and freshly milled black pepper

Step by step

Prepare the vinaigrette: Add the vinegar to the olive oil.

Add the chopped parsley, torn basil, lemon zest, lemon juice and garlic. Season then whisk thoroughly.

Cut the tomatoes in half and spread them with a little of the vinaigrette.

Place the tomatoes in the oven at 160C/Gas Mark 3 for two hours.

Place the peppers in a roasting tray or pan and grill them until their skins have blistered and blackened.

Allow the peppers to cool then peel off the skin, remove the seeds and cut into pieces.

Remove the tomatoes from the oven. Cut the vegetables into pieces, cover with vinaigrette and marinate for 20 minutes.

Heat a grill pan until the bars begin to smoke then grill the vegetables until nicely coloured.

Slice the mozzarella and then dip it into the remaining vinaigrette.

Layer the vegetables and mozzarella on individual plates.

For a more substantial meal, top this dish with salad leaves and serve it with crusty, fresh bread.

Fish dishes

We're so fortunate in Norfolk to be so close to the sea. It means that the fish we use is always as fresh as can be and we always have such a wide choice. At The Lavender House we get our fish from Gary Howard on Fye Bridge Street in Norwich, and depending on the time of year, he'll deliver everything from fresh Norfolk mussels, crab, lobster, mackerel, huss, pollock and cod – you name it, he's got it!

Once you've mastered the art of preparing fresh fish, cooking it is very simple; in fact, cooking the fish course can be the easiest part of the meal altogether.

Although delicious, due to the large chunk of fish immersed in hot liquid, this soup can be rather difficult to eat. My advice is to throw etiquette out of the window and tuck your serviette tightly under your chin alternatively a nice, tomato-coloured shirt or crimson blouse should do the trick!

Ingredients

Serves four

1kg assorted fish
2 leeks
1 large onion
1 bulb fennel
3 carrots, diced
4 cloves garlic
6 tomatoes, peeled and de-seeded
1 tablespoon tomato purée
Olive oil for frying
1 bay leaf
1 teaspoon cayenne pepper

1 litre water
2 glasses dry white wine
3 medium-sized potatoes, peeled and diced
Pinch saffron
Mayonnaise
Grated Gruyère cheese

For the croutons
4 slices crusty bread
2 cloves garlic
1 tablespoon olive oil

Step by step

1 Finely dice the leeks, celery, carrots and garlic cloves.

2 Fry these in hot olive oil.

3 Add the cayenne pepper and tomato purée and fry for two more minutes.

4 Add the tomato flesh, potato dice, water, wine, bay leaf and thyme.

5 Add the saffron and bring to the boil then simmer for 10 minutes.

6 Cut the fish into chunks and place in the pot with some fennel slices.

7 Bring to the boil and simmer for five minutes.

8 **Make the croutons:** Rub the bread with the remaining garlic then grill it on both sides.

9 Remove from the grill and drizzle with olive oil.

10 Place the stew in a bowl and decorate with the fennel tops. Serve with the garlic croutons, Gruyère cheese and mayonnaise.

Try using a selection of fish such as dogfish, skate, monktail, haddock, mackerel, salmon and mussels.

Cromer is famous for its crab which is readily available during the summer. At The Lavender House we get our crabs from Kevin Jonas - you couldn't get a better name for a fisherman! This makes a lovely, light lunch and goes well with salad and home-made garlic mayonnaise.

Ingredients

Serves four

2 decent-sized dressed crabs
165g can sweetcorn
165g white breadcrumbs
Small piece red pepper
Small bunch flat-leaf parsley
½ small red chilli (optional)
Juice of ½ lemon
1 egg
25g butter
1 teaspoon olive oil
Pinch salt

Step by step

Crush the sweetcorn in a blender.

Place the corn and crabmeat in a bowl.

Add the breadcrumbs and mix well.

Dice the red pepper and chop the parsley.

Add the pepper and parsley to the crab and corn mixture.

Bind the mixture with the lemon juice.

Add the egg and a pinch of salt, then add more breadcrumbs if necessary.

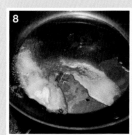
Heat the butter and olive oil together.

Place spoonfuls of the crab mixture into the pan and cook for a couple of minutes on either side.

Decorate with lemon wedges and flat-leaf parsley.

These would go well with a salsa, like the one served with the chilli, chickpea and coriander cakes.

This looks very attractive thanks to the fact that the fish is piled high on top of the potato, making it a real restaurant dish. If you haven't got any paprika in the cupboard, you could put some turmeric or saffron threads through the mayonnaise to ensure that it has some colour.

Ingredients

Serves four

4 pieces salmon fillet
10 small new potatoes
2 cloves garlic
3 tablespoons mayonnaise
½ teaspoon smoked paprika
50g butter
Zest and juice of ½ lemon
Small bunch chives

Step by step

1 Boil the new potatoes until cooked (around 15 minutes).

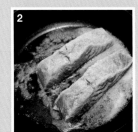

2 Dust the salmon with the flour then heat the butter and fry the fish skin-side down for a couple of minutes.

3 Turn the heat down and cook the fish on the other side for a couple more minutes.

4 Chop the chives and mix with the lemon zest.

5 Crush the cooked potatoes with the top of a rolling pin.

6 Add the chives and the lemon zest.

7 Add the lemon juice then season well.

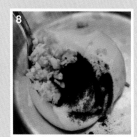

8 Crush the garlic and add this and the paprika to the mayonnaise.

9 To serve, pile the crushed potatoes into a pastry cutter then remove the ring.

10 Top with the salmon and mayonnaise and decorate with chives.

Leaving the skin on the salmon when frying it will give this dish a lovely, crispy texture.

This is a great celebratory dish as it can be prepared a few days in advance and has a real wow factor. The best way to make it is with long sliced smoked salmon rather than the cheap variety or it won't taste very different from the plastic that separates the layers of fish!

Ingredients

Makes 12 portions (freezable)

8 long slices smoked salmon
8 cooked asparagus spears
8 cooked small new potatoes, chopped
125g butter
1 lemon
1 teaspoon horseradish
Small bunch flat-leaf parsley
Freshly ground black pepper
Slices of fresh granary bread

Step by step

Line a loaf tin with clingfilm.

Cook the asparagus spears in boiling water.

Roughly chop the flat-leaf parsley and the lemon zest.

Soften the butter, add plenty of pepper then stir in the parsley and lemon zest.

Add the horseradish and the lemon juice and beat well.

Line the tin with smoked salmon then dot some of the butter mix on top.

Place the asparagus on top. Repeat with more salmon, butter and the potatoes until you have used all the salmon.

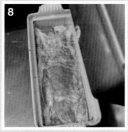

Fold the clingfilm over the terrine and press down firmly.

Place the terrine in the fridge for at least 30 minutes then turn it out and slice.

Serve the dish at room temperature with the slices of granary bread.

Alter this dish as you wish, perhaps with some fresh tarragon, sweet peppers or even fresh ginger.

This is a popular starter at The Lavender House and its lovely aroma will fill the kitchen when you're making it. Be careful not to overcook the scallops otherwise they'll be tough — if they're really fresh you shouldn't have any problems. Most supermarkets will sell ready-made polenta.

Ingredients

Serves four

8 scallops
100g ready-made polenta
4 rashers dry-cured streaky bacon
Juice of 1 lemon
Handful parsley
1 dessertspoon olive oil

Step by step

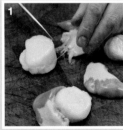

1 Trim the fish then remove the roe from the scallops. Set the scallops and roe aside.

2 Slice the polenta.

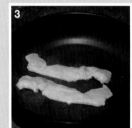

3 Heat a heavy-bottomed frying pan and fry the bacon.

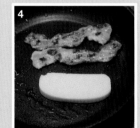

4 When the bacon is nearly cooked, place the slices of polenta into the pan.

5 Place the scallops and roe into the pan and cook for three minutes.

6 Chop the parsley.

7 Place the scallop roe on a plate, then the polenta and then the scallops.

8 Top with a piece of the fried bacon.

9 Add the olive oil, lemon juice and parsley to the pan and return this to the hob.

10 Cook until the mixture is hot then pour some sauce over each dish and serve.

You can vary this dish by using different herbs, such as mint or tarragon, for example.

A proper quiche should have a decent amount of filling. Fill this tart to the brim with lightly cooked, plump fish (the custard should simply hold the main ingredients in place), and when it's cooking, leave it slightly runny so the filling oozes out when it's cut.

Ingredients

Makes a 20cm tart. Serves four (freezable)

For the pastry

300g plain flour

175g butter

1 egg

Pinch salt

For the filling

150g fresh salmon fillet

50g smoked salmon

3 medium-sized free-range eggs

100ml whipping cream

150ml sour cream

5 spring onions

3 ripe tomatoes

Small bunch flat-leaf parsley

Salt and pepper

Step by step

1 Poach the fresh salmon fillet in a little water until the fish is just cooked (around five minutes).

2 **Make the pastry:** Rub the butter into the sifted flour and salt.

3 Add the egg and a little water and knead the mixture gently to form a smooth dough.

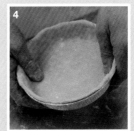

4 Roll out the pastry and line a greased flan tin. Prick the bottom with a fork.

5 **Make the filling:** First, chop the washed spring onions.

6 Remove the seeds from the tomatoes and chop the flesh.

7 Add the poached salmon and the chopped parsley.

8 Add the sour cream and whipping cream, beat in the eggs then season.

9 Gently pour the filling into the pastry case then place the smoked salmon on top.

10 Cook at 200C/Gas Mark 6 for 25 minutes until the filling has set.

Real men don't eat quiche apparently, so let's call this a tart then everyone can enjoy a slice!

Samphire is a delicious vegetable which grows on the coastal marshes in the north of the county. It is in season from June to September, and during this time is readily available in North Norfolk. You can buy it from one of the many roadside stalls that dot the North Norfolk coast.

Ingredients

Serves four

4 x 125g haddock
200g samphire
4 eggs
50g plain flour
100g butter
Splash white wine vinegar
Black pepper

Step by step

Toss the fish in the flour until coated.

Spread the butter on to a baking tray then place the fish on the tray. Bake at 180C/Gas Mark 4 for 15 minutes.

Cook the samphire in boiling, salted water for three minutes.

Strain the samphire and remove any stalks.

Add a little butter and some black pepper to the samphire.

Put the water and white wine vinegar in a saucepan and bring to the boil.

Whisk the water up until it whirls then break in the eggs.

Poach the eggs for two to three minutes.

Place the samphire on the plates and top with the fish.

Add the poached eggs and serve.

The idea of this is that when you break the poached egg it will form a sauce for the dish.

You can either cook the pieces of fish individually, roast them on a baking tray or fry them in several frying pans to cook them all at once. Skate goes very well with lemon and garlic butter, and perfect accompaniments for this include new potatoes and green or broad beans.

Ingredients

Serves four

4 skate wings
1 lemon
2 cloves garlic
200g butter
50g plain flour
Handful flat-leaf parsley
Salt and pepper

Step by step

Prepare the fish by trimming the back bone.

Season the flour then use it to coat the fish.

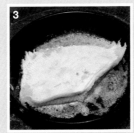
Melt the butter in a heavy-based frying pan then fry the fish for a couple of minutes.

Turn the fish over and cook for a couple more minutes.

Chop the garlic.

Add the garlic to the frying pan.

Add the butter.

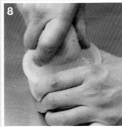
Squeeze the lemon juice.

Chop the parsley and add this and the lemon juice to the pan.

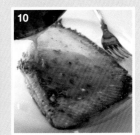
Place the fish on the plates, heat the butter sauce again then pour this over the fish and serve immediately.

You may find you need to cook the fish for a little longer; it depends on the thickness of the skate.

This particular salad works very well with the mackerel as it complements oily fish very nicely. You can also serve it with other oily or smoked fish such as herring, trout or salmon. To make a more substantial dish, boil and crush some new potatoes and add them to the salad.

Ingredients

Serves four

4 good-sized mackerel fillets
½ teaspoon English mustard
50g gherkins
25g capers
1 large red apple
1 small red onion
1 teaspooon sea salt
Small bunch tarragon
1 tablespoon natural yoghurt
1 tablespoon olive oil

Step by step

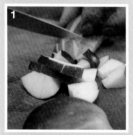

Chop the apple into pieces, leaving the skin on the fruit.

Chop the tarragon and add it to the apple.

Dice and add the red apple then add the capers and mix well.

Chop the gherkins and add them to the mix.

Stir in the mustard.

Stir in the natural yoghurt and mix well.

Brush the fish with olive oil then sprinkle it with sea salt.

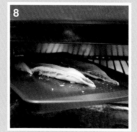

Grill the mackerel for around three minutes.

Put a few spoonfuls of salad on to each plate.

Top with the fish.

Mackerel is a great fish to work with as it's inexpensive and always available.

We make this dish during our fresh fish demonstrations which take place on a Saturday morning. It goes well with new potatoes and a green salad and is great for Sunday lunch as it looks like a roast joint of meat when it's done (remember to take the string off before serving!).

Ingredients

Serves four

750g whole monkfish tail or fresh monkfish fillets
2 cloves garlic
Handful parsley
3 bay leaves
2 lemons
25g capers
1 teaspoon olive oil

Step by step

Skin the monkfish tail and remove the bone, leaving 5cm of the tail bone.

Trim the sinew from the fish.

Make the gremolata: First, chop the garlic.

Chop the parsley and mix this with the garlic then add the chopped capers.

Remove the zest from the lemons and add this to the garlic and parsley mixture.

Squeeze the lemon juice and pour this in.

Pour three quarters of the mixture over the fish and spread evenly.

Place the bay leaves on top of the mixure.

Tie the fish up with string to keep it together.

Place the fish on a hot baking tray brushed with a little olive oil then roast in the oven at 180C/Gas Mark 4 for around 20 minutes.

If you don't fancy preparing the fish yourself you can buy ready-prepared monkfish fillets.

Traditionally this dish is made with cod but pollock tastes just as good and is very trendy at the moment; alternatively you can make it with haddock. It goes well with grilled tomatoes – just grill some tomato slices for a few minutes then drizzle them with olive oil.

Ingredients

Serves four

600g pollock
4 slices white bread, crusts cut off
1 lemon
50g Smoked Dapple or other hard cheese
50g butter
2 teaspoons horseradish
Handful parsley

Step by step

Trim the pollock.

Cut the fish into chunks.

Place the bread in the blender and blend until it turns into crumbs.

Squeeze the lemon juice over the fish.

Chop the parsley, spread this over the fish then leave to marinate.

Place the fish on a buttered baking tray.

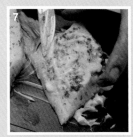

Spread the horseradish on top of the fish.

Grate the cheese and mix this with the breadcrumbs.

Top the fish with the cheese and breadcrumb mixture.

Dot the fish with a little butter then place in the oven at 200C/Gas Mark 6 for around 10 minutes.

For the best flavour, leave the fish to marinate for at least two hours.

We use St Peter's Best Bitter or Woodforde's Wherry for this but any bitter will do and you can even use lager if you want to. Huss is an unusual fish and is caught locally in the North Atlantic – it's sometimes sold as Rock Salmon. It's a little softer than monkfish or catfish.

Ingredients

Serves four

For the fish

600g huss
100ml bitter
125g plain flour
20g yeast
1 teaspoon sugar
Juice of ½ lemon

For the tartare sauce

4 tablespoons mayonnaise
1 teaspoon chopped onion
1 teaspoon chopped gherkin
1 teaspoon chopped parsley
1 teaspoon capers
Juice of ½ lemon
Wedges of lemon to serve

Step by step

Make the batter: Warm the beer.

Place the yeast and sugar in a bowl.

Pour the beer on to the yeast and sugar and stir until dissolved.

Add the flour then cover and set aside for 30 minutes.

Trim the fish and cut it into bite-sized pieces.

Marinate the fish in the lemon juice for 20 minutes or so.

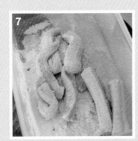

Toss the fish in the flour then dip it in the batter.

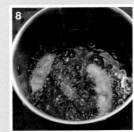

Deep-fry the fish for three or four minutes until it floats to the top and the batter is crisp and golden.

Make the tartare sauce: Mix together the onion, gherkins, capers and parsley then stir in the mayonnaise and lemon juice.

Pile the fish on to a plate and serve it with the tartare sauce and wedges of lemon.

You'll find that huss is an easy fish to fillet as it just has one big bone down the middle.

Nowadays you'll see fish pie on the trendiest of menus but families have been tucking into this classic for years. A word of warning, however; always make the pie double the size you think you'll need as it's a fabulous dish and so second helpings are almost obligatory!

Ingredients

Makes four big or six small portions

500g assorted fish (salmon, smoked haddock, prawns and smoked salmon)
125g spring onions
2 sticks celery
1 leek
2 tomatoes
100g butter
25g flour
250ml fish stock
500g potatoes suitable for mashing
1 egg yolk
100g grated smoked Norfolk Dapple or Cheddar
Salt and ground white pepper
Few sprigs parsley

Step by step

1. Boil the potatoes until soft. Drain them then return to the hob to remove excess moisture before mashing.

2. Finely chop the leek, celery and spring onions then fry them until soft in half the butter.

3. Add the flour. Stir in then cook for around three minutes.

4. Add the hot fish stock a ladle at a time, stirring constantly to give a smooth, silky sauce.

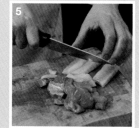

5. Ensure the fish is free of skin and bone. Cut it into bite-sized chunks.

6. Mix the fish with the shellfish then combine it with the sauce, adding an egg yolk.

7. Spoon the mixture into a deep, ovenproof dish.

8. Add the rest of the butter and the cheese then season well.

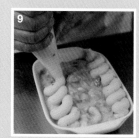

9. Pipe or spoon the mashed potato on top of the fish.

10. Bake the fish pie at 180C/Gas Mark 4 for 30 minutes until golden. Garnish with parsley.

Some people poach the fish first but, cut into small chunks, it will cook just as nicely in the sauce.

This dish is traditionally made with herrings but it works nicely with trout as well. There are lots of people in the Norfolk area who go trout fishing but who don't know what to do with the fish afterwards - this is a quick and easy solution and looks impressive, too.

Ingredients

Serves four

2 large trout
100g porridge oats
1 dessertspoon capers
25g flaked almonds
50g butter
1 egg
Squeeze lemon juice

Step by step

Fillet the trout.

Cut the fish into large chunks and coat it with the flour.

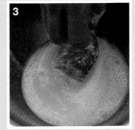

Beat the egg and dip the fish into it.

Cover the fish with oats.

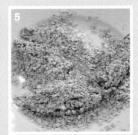

Make sure the fish is well coated then place it in a hot frying pan with a little butter.

Cook it for two to three minutes on either side.

Add another 50g butter and a dessertspoon of flaked almonds.

As the butter starts to foam and the almonds start to brown, add the capers.

Add the lemon juice.

Heat through then serve immediately.

You don't have to fillet the fish - you can keep it whole if you want to.

Moules marinières

There is something wonderfully decadent about a huge bowl of mussels. As there will be plenty of shells, large portions are essential, along with another bowl and maybe a bib! The done thing is to serve the mussels with a bowl of chips and some garlicky mayonnaise – absolutely delicious!

Ingredients

Makes four large portions

4kg fresh mussels
1kg onion, carrots and celery
1 bay leaf
Handful thyme
1 teaspoon black peppercorns
250ml double cream
1 large glass (250ml) white wine
1 large glass (250ml) water

Step by step

1. Scrub and scrape the mussels and discard any that are not tightly closed.

2. Bring the white wine and water to the boil.

3. Add the chopped vegetables, thyme and peppercorns then bring back to the boil.

4. Tip in the mussels and cover with a tight-fitting lid. Shake and stir frequently.

5. When the shells have opened (this should take around five minutes), strain through a colander into a pan.

6. Bring the liquid to a boil and reduce to half its volume. Add the cream. Bring to the boil and simmer for five minutes.

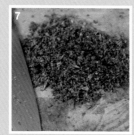

7. Chop the parsley.

8. Pour the creamy liquid over the mussels.

9. Garnish with the chopped parsley.

10. Serve immediately.

Norfolk mussels are finest in winter, small and juicy, combining sweetness with the tang of the sea.

Sea bass is a great barbecue dish, and if you go fishing off the coast you can cook it on the beach once you're back on dry land which is quite fun. If you do barbecue it, you'll need to wrap it in foil first before placing it on the barbecue - it should take around 20 minutes to cook.

Ingredients

Serves four

4 whole sea bass, around 350g each
1 lemon
4 large garlic cloves
Sea salt and black pepper
12 fresh bay leaves
1 dessertspoon olive oil

Step by step

Using a sharp knife, remove the scales from the sea bass.

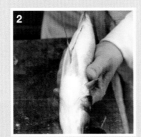

Take out the guts then wash the fish under the tap.

With the knife, score the fish quite deeply along its side.

Slice the lemon and stuff the fish with the lemon slices.

Cut the garlic cloves into large chunks and place these into, alongside and on top of the fish.

Grind some salt and pepper on top.

Place the fish on a baking tray and brush it generously with olive oil.

Place the bay leaves on top of the lemon slices then squeeze some lemon juice on top.

Bake the fish at 200C/Gas Mark 6 for 20 minutes.

Serve whole.

Farmed sea bass is readily available or you can buy it from the fishermen on the North Norfolk coast.

These burgers are a great way of getting children to eat fish and the good news is that they're far healthier than traditional meat-based burgers. If you do have tiny mouths to feed, simply make the tuna burgers smaller and leave out the salsa; just serve them in some soft, little buns.

Ingredients

Makes four (freezable)

400g fresh tuna
1 small pineapple
1 small red onion
Zest and juice of ½ lime
1 dessertspoon chopped coriander
1 small chilli, red or green
1 tablespoon plain flour
Pinch sea salt
Coarse black pepper
1 dessertspoon olive oil
4 burger buns

Step by step

Cut the tuna into small, square chunks.

Dice the red onion.

Place the tuna and half the onion into a food processor then season.

Pulse for two minutes, scrape down then pulse for a further minute.

Using the flour, shape the mixture into patties.

Make the salsa: Finely dice the pineapple.

Add the chilli and the lime zest.

Chop the fresh coriander then season.

In a bowl, add the lime juice, a splash of the olive oil and the rest of the onion.

Brush the burgers with olive oil and place on a griddle pan or barbecue for around three minutes each side.

These look good topped with the salsa and served on interesting buns such as olive or ciabatta.

This dish can also be made with fresh tuna or even with shark if you can get it. It has a summery, Mediterranean feel and is delicious hot or cold. As the dish already includes salad items, it would go well with a simple potato salad or with a small bowl of hot or cold couscous.

Ingredients

Serves four

600g fresh swordfish steak
100g rocket
50g pitted, marinated olives
3 tablespoons seasoned flour
3 dessertspoons olive oil
1 small English onion
2 ripe plum tomatoes
Freshly milled salt and pepper

Step by step

Trim the fish and cut it into sizeable chunks.

Roll the fish in the seasoned flour.

Place the olive oil and butter in the pan and, when hot, add the fish. Sauté for three to four minutes.

Finely chop the onion.

Add the onion dice to the swordfish.

Chop the tomatoes into quarters and add these to the pan.

Add the olives.

Add the rocket.

Season well.

Drizzle with olive oil and serve immediately.

If you're having an informal evening with friends or family, you could serve this dish in the pan.

Lobster has a lovely flavour and is readily available during the summer months (the lobster we use at The Lavender House comes from Sheringham). It looks rather complicated to do but don't be put off as when you've prepared a lobster once you'll soon get the hang of it for another time.

Ingredients

Serves four

2 x 1.25kg cooked lobsters
Handful rocket
1 lemon

Step by step

1. First, take the lobster and break off the claws.

2. Slice the lobster down the middle.

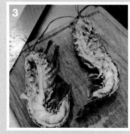

3. Use a sharp knife to break it in half.

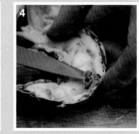

4. Remove the legs and the tract.

5. Lift out the tail meat, slice it then lay it back in the lobster shell.

6. Break the claws at the joints with your knife.

7. Use the back of your knife to gently break the base of each claw.

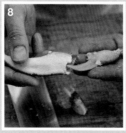

8. Push out the lobster meat with your fingers.

9. Gather up all the lobster pieces and place them on a plate.

10. Garnish with the lemon and rocket.

As lobster has such a delicate flavour it's best to keep it simple and just serve it with some lemon.

As this mackerel dish comes with pickled vegetables, you really don't need any more to accompany it; instead, simply serve it with some slices of really good, fresh bread. At The Lavender House this is served as a starter but it also makes a great main course or a simple lunch.

Ingredients

Serves four

Four fresh mackerel
250ml water
100ml white wine vinegar
1 star anise
6 peppercorns
½ teaspoon fennel seeds
6 slices fresh red chilli
1 teaspoon caster sugar
Handful wild mushrooms
1 carrot
1 courgette
½ onion
2 dessertspoons olive oil
2 dessertspoons lemon juice
Handful sea salt

Step by step

Pour the water and white wine vinegar into a saucepan and add the star anise, peppercorns and fennel seeds.

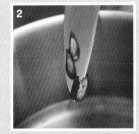

Add the chilli to the pan.

Add the sugar and bring it up to the boil.

Peel the carrot and courgette and slice the onion and the mushrooms.

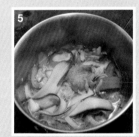

Place all the vegetables in the water and return the pan to the heat for one minute.

Take the vegetables out of the hot water and plunge them in cold water.

Fillet the mackerel.

Score the fish and sprinkle it with coarse sea salt.

Brush the fish with olive oil and place it on a baking tray.

Place the vegetables on the plates and top with the fish. Sprinkle on some of the pickling liquor and serve.

If you don't fancy filleting the mackerel, buy it ready done or serve it whole.

Main courses

Making main courses is something I love to do, perhaps because meat can be so forgiving. What I mean is that when you bake, or make desserts or petits fours, you need to be very precise and weigh out all the ingredients carefully. But with main courses you can follow your instincts a little more, adding a pinch of this and a spoonful of that.

As you'll see from the tips on the following pages, you can cook the meat according to how you and your guests like it, and ring the changes with a sprinkling of fresh herbs, and by adding different side dishes and accompaniments.

Despite today's state-of-the-art kitchens, many of us are still seduced by the thought of cooking alfresco on hot coals. Often it's something simple that works best on a barbecue, such as this favourite of mine, Thai chicken satay, whose tasty peanut sauce children seem to love.

Ingredients
Makes eight sticks

For the barbecue chicken
Eight large chicken thigh fillets
2 cloves garlic
2 teaspoons finely sliced lemon grass
2 teaspoons crushed, fresh ginger
One small, fresh chilli
Pinch cracked black peppercorns
1 tablespoon sweet soy sauce

Juice of 1 lemon
1 tablespoon finely chopped coriander
For the peanut sauce
300g peanut butter
400ml can coconut milk
1 tablespoon tamarind paste
2 tablespoons sweet chilli sauce
1 tablespoon brown sugar

Step by step

1 Bone the chicken thighs and trim off the excess fat and skin.

2 Place the chicken in a bowl then add the peppercorns and the soy sauce.

3 Add the chopped coriander and the lemon grass.

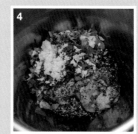

4 Chop the garlic and ginger, slice the chilli and add to the chicken with the lemon juice. Marinate for an hour.

5 Thread the chicken pieces on to skewers.

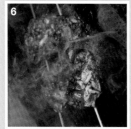

6 Cook the chicken on the barbecue or under the grill, turning frequently.

7 **Prepare the peanut sauce:** Place the peanut butter, chilli sauce and sugar in a bowl.

8 Add the tamarind paste.

9 Add the coconut milk and a little hot water.

Stir well then serve the sauce alongside the cooked chicken.

Boning the chicken cuts down on cooking time and ensures a successful, safe afternoon barbecue.

This classic confit from the Dordogne region of France combines delightfully with pieces of mango to introduce some much-needed sunshine into our lives. The confit de canard works well whether your ducks are Barbarys from Perigueux or good, old Norfolks from Hingham.

Ingredients

Serves four

4 large duck legs
Handful sea salt
1kg lard or goose fat
500g honey
2 fresh, ripe mangos
2 small red onions
Juice of 2 lemons
Zest and juice of 2 limes
2 dessertspoons white wine vinegar
100g fresh ginger
2 bay leaves
1 whole garlic bulb
1 large bunch flat-leaf parsley, chopped
Black pepper
Handful salad leaves

Step by step

Rub the duck legs with the salt and leave for two hours, then wipe them with a dry cloth.

Place in a deep tray, add the bay leaves and garlic (sliced in half) and cover with melted fat.

Cook at 150C/Gas Mark 2 for around four hours.

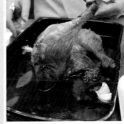

Remove the duck legs from the fat and drain them well.

Turn the oven to 200C/ Gas Mark 6. Place the legs on a baking tray and drizzle with honey. Cook for 20 minutes.

Make the salsa:
Dice the mangos, red onions and ginger then add the lime zest.

Place in a mixing bowl and add the lime juice.

Add the lemon juice, wine vinegar, a pinch of salt and plenty of freshly-milled pepper.

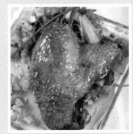

Place the duck on an attractive serving dish.

Garnish with dressed salad leaves and surround with the salsa.

The glorious thing about this confit is that once it's cooked it will keep, covered in fat, for weeks.

If you're used to bottled Caesar salad dressing, you'll find this as different as can be, dressing crunchy leaves in a delicate yet delicious manner. Invented in 1928 by Caesar Cardini, an Italian who worked in a chic establishment in Tijuana, Mexico, this appears on menus worldwide.

Ingredients

Serves four

2 chicken breasts
2 heads romaine lettuce
2 white rolls
100g butter
2 cloves garlic
1 egg
Squeeze lemon juice
Dash Worcester sauce
10 silver skin anchovy fillets
125ml light olive oil
100g Parmesan shavings
Salt and freshly milled black pepper

Step by step

1 Cook the chicken breasts on a griddle pan for 10 to 15 minutes.

2 Cut the bread into chunks then fry it in butter along with the chopped garlic.

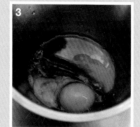

3 Place the egg, lemon juice, Worcester sauce and five anchovy fillets into a bowl.

4 Blend at full speed with a hand blender or in a food processor.

5 With the blender still running, slowly add the olive oil.

6 Wash and dry the romaine lettuce and tear it into pieces.

7 Pour on the Caesar dressing and mix well.

8 Add the croutons and the remaining whole anchovy fillets.

9 Add the Parmesan shavings, season and then toss the ingredients together.

10 Place the salad in a large bowl then top with the grilled chicken.

My Head Chef, Richard Knights, worked in America for 18 months and made this almost every day!

The restaurant may be non-smoking, but this doesn't apply to the kitchen. No, we haven't started puffing in the car park; the clouds of aromatic smoke are generated by our latest invention, a home smoker made from a battered roasting tin, a pastry cooling rack and a roll of cooking foil!

Ingredients

Serves four

4 chicken breasts, free of bone with the skin on
2 dessertspoons olive oil
1 lemon
1 teaspoon fresh, chopped garlic
Pinch dried chilli
1 teaspoon sea salt
Few sprigs fresh rosemary
Few sprigs fresh lavender
Freshly milled black pepper
1 bag wood smoking chips

Step by step

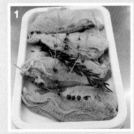

Put the chicken breasts into a deep dish with the sea salt, rosemary and lavender.

Add the olive oil, lemon juice and zest and the black pepper.

Refrigerate the chicken for four hours or, even better, overnight.

Soak half the wood chips in water and spread the rest across the bottom of a deep, heavy roasting tin.

Add the soaked wood chips to the dry chips.

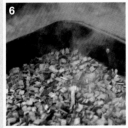

Cover the tray with foil and warm it over a low heat until the chips start to smoke.

Place the chicken on a rack on top of the tray and cover it with foil.

Cook the chicken in the oven for 30 minutes at 180C/Gas Mark 4 until golden.

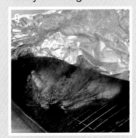

Carefully remove the foil, allowing the smoke to escape (it's a good idea to do this outside).

You can serve the chicken hot or cold.

This goes well with a classic Waldorf salad or served on crusty bread spread with mayonnaise.

Belly of pork is quite an inexpensive cut but it's very trendy at the moment and you'll see it everywhere (it's featured on the menus at all our restaurants). The meat can be a little fatty but when it's cooked properly it renders down. It goes well with parsnips, cabbage and greens.

Ingredients

Serves four

1kg pork belly
1 garlic clove
1 good-sized piece fresh ginger
1 small red chilli
½ teaspoon black peppercorns
2 cloves
Pinch cumin
2 cardamon seeds
1 dessertspoon honey
½ teaspoon tamarind paste (optional)
1 large onion
250ml water
Coarsely ground sea salt

Step by step

Remove the skin from the pork and set this aside.

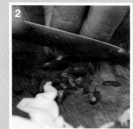

Chop the garlic, ginger and chilli.

Place the garlic, ginger and chilli in a pestal and mortar and grind together, along with the black peppercorns.

Add the cloves, cumin and cardamon seeds and continue grinding then add the honey and grind again.

Slice the onion and place this in a dry pan or roasting tin.

Place the pork on top of the onion slices.

Spread the spicy paste on top of the meat and pour on the water.

Place the skin on top of the marinade.

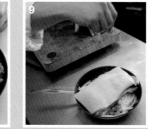

Sprinkle with salt, cover with foil then cook at 220C/Gas Mark 8 for 30 minutes. Reduce the oven to 160C/Gas Mark 3 and cook for 3 hours.

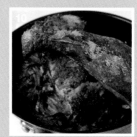

Pile the onions on to the plates and place the pieces of pork on top, with some crackling on the side.

If you're not used to preparing meat, your butcher will be happy to take the skin off the pork for you.

This lovely dish is another of my favourites and doesn't take long to prepare. The pork we use comes from D.J. Barnard in Attleborough and has a great flavour. Serve this with rice or a crisp, green salad, then treat yourself to a glass or two of well-deserved wine.

Ingredients

Serves four

2 pork tenderloins
1 teaspoon plain flour
1 teaspoon smoked paprika
1 x 400g can cooked butter beans
100g chorizo
100ml natural yoghurt
100ml double cream
50g butter
Large bunch flat-leaf parsley

Step by step

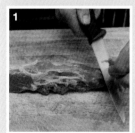
Trim the pork fillet.

Slice the meat and place it in a bowl.

Coat the pork with the paprika and the flour.

Heat the butter until it starts to foam.

Add the pork and cook for four to five minutes.

Slice the chorizo and add this to the pan.

Add the butter beans.

Take the pan off the heat and stir in the yoghurt and the cream.

Add most of the chopped parsley.

Place several spoonfuls of the mixture on to plates or shallow bowls then decorate it with the remaining parsley.

You can swap the chorizo for some locally-made sausage or even some black pudding.

This dish is a throwback to the 1980s when it was considered to be cutting edge. Gammon is quite salty and can be a little difficult to digest, which is why the pineapple is such a good accompaniment. We serve this at The Pigs pub in Edgefield and it goes really well with chunky chips.

Ingredients

Serves four

1kg gammon joint
1 small, ripe pineapple
2 dessertspoons honey
¼ teaspoon dried chillies
50g butter

Step by step

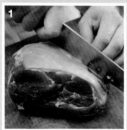

1 Score the top of the gammon with a sharp knife and tie the meat with string if necessary.

2 Put the butter in a saucepan or roasting tray and place the gammon in the pan.

3 Pour the honey on top of the gammon.

4 Sprinkle with the dried chillies.

5 Place the meat in the oven at 200C/Gas Mark 6 and cook for 45 minutes.

6 Top and tail the fresh pineapple and remove the skin.

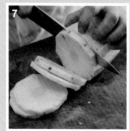

7 Cut the pineapple into fairly thick slices.

8 When the joint is cooked, remove it from the pan and put in the pineapple slices.

9 Return the meat to the oven and cook it again for at least 45 minutes.

Slice the gammon and place it on a plate with the pineapple.

This is a great dish to serve up on a cold day and goes well with Boston baked beans.

This barbecue sauce is a real winner. It goes well with all manner of grilled meats and even brushed on to corn cobs. If you increase the quantity of the ingredients, you can make some extra sauce to keep in the fridge; that way you can make this quickly another day.

Ingredients

Serves four

4 pork chops
4 shallots or 1 English onion
150ml soy sauce
1 tablespoon tomato purée
Small piece fresh ginger
5 cloves garlic
1 tablespoon honey
1 tablespoon mustard powder
1 large red chilli
1 tablespoon Jack Daniels
2 tablespoons soft brown sugar
3 tablespoons water
Handful salad leaves

Step by step

1
Slice the garlic.

2
Dice the red chilli.

3
Dice the onion.

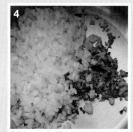
4
Mix the garlic, chilli and onion together and place them in a pan.

5
Add the brown sugar and the honey.

6
Place on the hob and cook until the onions are soft then add the mustard powder and the soy sauce.

7
Pour in the Jack Daniels and the water then simmer for a few minutes.

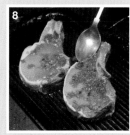
8
Place the pork chops on to a grill pan or griddle and coat with the sauce. Grill until just cooked.

Spoon some more barbecue sauce over the chops.

Decorate with salad leaves and serve.

Try serving some extra sauce on the side (we use our tiny copper pans for this).

We used to make this when I was at Rookery Hall, near Nantwich in Cheshire, in the early 1980s. When I was there we had all sorts of celebrity guests including Margaret Thatcher and Robert Maxwell. It's a stunning place and it was next to the Rolls-Royce factory – very swish!

Ingredients

Serves four

4 duck breasts
1 dessertspoon pure maple syrup
1 onion
125g stoneless prunes
Coarsely milled salt and black pepper
250ml chicken stock
1 dessertspoon brandy
1 orange

Step by step

1 Trim some of the excess fat off the duck breasts then score the meat with a sharp knife.

2 Season well then place the duck skin-side down in a hot, dry pan until the skin is crisp. Add the maple syrup.

3 Dice the onion.

4 Tip the fat away from the pan, turn the meat over and add the onion.

5 Add the prunes to the pan then cook for another five minutes.

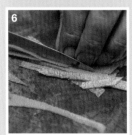

6 Chop up the orange zest (a dessertspoonful will be fine).

7 Add this to the pan, together with the brandy then ignite the brandy.

8 Remove the duck from the pan and set it aside.

9 Add the stock to the pan, swirl it around then reduce down.

10 Place some of the prune mixture on each plate, slice the duck breast and place this on top. Decorate with orange segments and serve.

You could use a whole duck for this dish and keep the legs for the confit recipe featured earlier.

This dish always goes down well during our cookery demonstrations as it's quick and easy but also impressive. A lot of men come along to the demos and they tend to like the meat dishes. Serving it with pancakes as well makes a small amount of steak go a long way.

Ingredients

Serves four

For the beef

500g prepared beef fillet
125g soft butter
½ teaspoon cracked black peppercorns
½ teaspoon fresh rosemary
1 dessertspoon olive oil

For the horseradish pancakes

125g plain flour
1 dessertspoon horseradish
½ teaspoon baking powder
125ml milk
1 egg
Salt and pepper

Step by step

Prepare the butter: Mix the rosemary and pepper with the softened butter.

Roll the mixture up in greaseproof paper and place it in the fridge.

Make the pancake mixture: Place the flour, baking powder, egg and milk in a bowl.

Whisk to form a stiff batter.

Add the horseradish and the salt and pepper.

Cut the beef into slices around 1cm thick.

Heat some olive oil in a frying pan then flash-fry the meat for a minute each side (or longer, depending on how you like it).

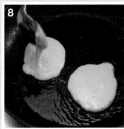

Place spoonfuls of the pancake mixture into the frying pan.

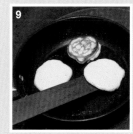

Cook for one minute on each side.

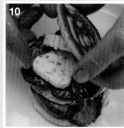

Place a pancake on a plate followed by a piece of beef, then some butter. Top with another pancake then drizzle with more butter.

Cauliflower fritters, stuffed onions and courgette, mozzarella and tomato bake all go well with this.

This is a nice, succulent dish and is a great way to warm up after a bracing Sunday walk. You can bake it in the oven without the water but if you do it'll be much drier as the water steams it and prevents it from drying out. Or place the pan on the hob and cook it that way.

Ingredients

Serves four (freezable)

2 middle neck fillets of lamb
100g redcurrant jelly
100g shredded suet
100g baby onions
200g plain flour
1 dessertspoon olive oil
1 teaspoon baking powder
2 dessertspoons lamb stock
Pinch dried tarragon
Pinch chopped rosemary
Pinch salt

Step by step

1 Trim the lamb and cut it into chunks.

2 Place a teaspoon of flour in a bowl, add the lamb and coat it with the flour.

3 Add the tarragon and mix well.

4 Pour the olive oil into the pan then fry the lamb for a few minutes to seal it.

5 Stir in the onions, the redcurrant jelly and the stock then take the pan off the heat and leave it to cool.

6 Make the pastry: Place the suet, flour and rosemary in a bowl then add the salt and baking powder.

7 Bind the mixture with a little cold water, knead it on a floured surface then roll it out with a rolling pin.

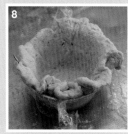

8 Line the pudding tins with clingfilm followed by the suet pastry, leaving a little around the edges.

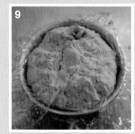

9 Fill the puddings with the lamb mixture then mould the pastry tops together with your fingertips.

10 Half-fill a roasting tin with water, place the puddings in the tray, cover with foil and bake at 180C/Gas Mark 4 for two hours.

You can make one large pudding but if you do you'll need to add an hour to the cooking time.

We used to have this every Thursday for tea when I was a child (we always had the same things on the same days of the week!). It's a lovely dish and works well in a hurry as it's very easy to make. In fact, it's the ultimate fast food as it only takes five minutes from start to finish.

Ingredients

Serves four

For the lamb's liver

500g lamb's liver
125ml lamb stock
100g bacon
1 teaspoon plain flour
25g butter
1 onion
1 tomato
Good bunch parsley

For the mustard mash

600g peeled potatoes
50g butter
1 dessertspoon mild English mustard
Salt and pepper

Step by step

1 **Make the mustard mash:** Peel and halve the potatoes then boil until soft.

2 Drain the potatoes, return to the hob to remove the excess moisture then mash them with the mustard and butter.

3 Cut the lamb's liver into bite-sized chunks then coat the meat with the flour.

4 Put the butter in a frying pan, add the lamb's liver and cook for three minutes.

5 Set aside.

6 Slice the onion and place it in a dry pan. Chop the bacon into lardons and add these to the onion.

7 Remove the flesh from the tomato and cut it into quarters.

8 Add the tomato pieces to the onion and bacon mixture.

9 Make up the lamb stock and add this to the pan.

Spoon some mash on the plates, top with the meat and surround with the sauce. Garnish with parsley.

If you like your meat pink, just fry this for a minute or two; a little longer for meat that's well done.

This is a really old-fashioned dish and I always feel as if I'm going back in time when I eat it because as a child I always used to have corned beef hash after football practice. It's incredibly popular with our customers at The Pigs pub in Edgefield and the staff there love it, too.

Ingredients

Serves four

340g tin corned beef
200g chopped tomatoes
1kg Maris Piper potatoes
1 dessertspoon Colman's mustard
Sprig of fresh thyme
4 spring onions
1 duck's egg
Freshly ground salt and pepper
Pinch grated nutmeg

Step by step

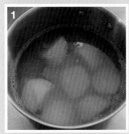

1. Bring the potatoes to the boil and boil until soft.

2. Drain the potatoes then return them to the hob to remove any excess moisture. Add the mustard, then mash.

3. Pick the thyme and add this to the mash.

4. Chop and add the spring onions.

5. Season well with salt and pepper then leave to cool.

6. Stir in the corned beef.

7. Place the chopped tomatoes in the bottom of a suitable serving dish and top with the corned beef mixture.

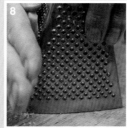

8. Grate the cheese and place this on top then cook at 180C/Gas Mark 4 for 20 minutes.

9. Melt the butter in a frying pan and add the spinach. Season with salt, pepper and nutmeg.

Fry the egg. Take the corned beef hash out of the oven and place the spinach and the fried egg on top.

You can leave the corned beef mixture to go cold then make it into hash cakes for breakfast.

The caraway dumplings used in this dish are similar to traditional Norfolk dumplings, just with a caraway twist (for something different another time you can also use other flavourings such as fennel seeds). And if you haven't got beef dripping, simply use vegetable oil or lard instead.

Ingredients

Serves four (freezable)

For the goulash

500g diced casserole beef (topside)
50g beef dripping
250g beef stock
125g baby onions
1 stick celery
1 carrot
1 teaspoon tomato purée
1 teaspoon paprika
Small bunch chives
2 dessertspoons sour cream or natural yoghurt

For the dumplings

100g self-raising flour
½ teaspoon baking powder
50g suet
½ teaspoon salt
1 teaspoon caraway seeds
Cold water to bind

Step by step

Peel, trim and dice the celery and carrot.

Add the baby onions.

Place the diced beef in a bowl then coat the meat with the flour and paprika.

Melt the beef dripping in a frying pan and seal the beef.

Add the celery, carrot and onion mixture and fry for five minutes until the beef is nicely coloured.

Make up the beef stock and add this to the pan followed by the tomato purée. Mix well.

Cover the pan with foil and place it in the oven at 180C/Gas Mark 4 for three hours.

Make the dumplings: Place the flour, baking powder and suet in a bowl, add the caraway seeds and the cold water and bind together.

When the casserole has cooked for two-and-a-half hours, add the dumplings then return it to the oven for a further half an hour.

Chop the chives, whip the sour cream or yoghurt then use these to garnish the goulash.

You can use regular diced onion in this dish but I prefer to use whole baby onions as they look great.

Cornish pasties make perfect convenience food as not only do they taste great but they're a lot better for you than snacks such as burgers and fries. We're often asked to make these when we hold the men-only cookery classes at The Lavender House and they always go down well.

Ingredients

Serves four (freezable)

400g skirt of beef
250g plain flour
125g lard
1 large carrot
1 onion
1 swede
1 egg
1 teaspoon thyme
Pinch salt
Pinch freshly ground black pepper

Step by step

Dice the carrot, swede and onion and place these in a bowl.

Chop the beef into cubes.

Add the beef to the vegetable dice.

Add the flour then mix well.

Add the thyme then season with salt and pepper.

Make the pastry:
Place the flour and salt in a bowl then rub in the lard.

Bind with cold water then roll the pastry out on a floured surface.

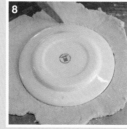

Place a side plate on top of the pastry and cut round it to make circles.

Put some water around the edge of the pastry circles, place some of the filling mixture in the middle then pinch the edges together.

Put the pasties on a baking tray, brush them with beaten egg then bake at 180C/Gas Mark 4 for 50 minutes.

Cornish pasties taste great hot or cold so are perfect for packing up to take to work or on a journey.

This recipe comes from the 1960s when The Lavender House was called The Old Beams and, as fashion comes round again, dishes such as this are back in favour. This was a dish that the "old school" waiters would cook at the table, making for great theatre and customers loved it!

Ingredients

Serves four

800g fillet steak
200g button mushrooms
2 teaspoons olive oil
2 teaspoons Dijon mustard
100ml brandy
½ onion
2 teaspoons Worcester sauce
250ml whipping or double cream
Freshly ground salt and pepper
2 tablespoons chopped chives

Step by step

Cut the beef into medallions.

Seal the beef in a little olive oil.

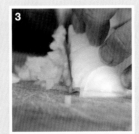

Chop the onion.

Slice the mushrooms.

Add the mushrooms and onion to the pan then fry for a couple of minutes.

Pour in the brandy.

Ignite the brandy then stir well.

Take the beef out of the pan then cover it with foil to keep it warm.

Add the mustard and Worcester sauce to the pan then stir in the cream.

Place the sauce on the plates, top with the beef and sprinkle on the chives.

If you prefer your steak well done, just leave it in the pan for an extra minute or two.

This tasty tart reminds me of sunny French bistros. Ready-made puff pastry is easy to come by these days, but try to buy a version that's been made with butter as this will make a huge difference to the dish. Serve it with a crisp, green salad for a light lunch, or take slices on a picnic.

Ingredients

Serves four

1kg red onions
125g puff pastry
Zest of 1 small orange
Splash olive oil
1 dessertspoon granulated sugar
2 dessertspoons white wine vinegar
Pinch fresh thyme
25g black olives
25g shaved Parmesan
25g silver skin anchovies

Step by step

1. Peel and finely slice the red onions.

2. Add the orange zest.

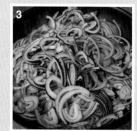

3. Place the onions, orange zest and thyme into a pan and soften over a low heat.

4. Add the sugar and the vinegar.

5. Simmer gently, stirring frequently until the liquid has evaporated and the onions are sticky (around 30 minutes).

6. Roll the puff pastry out into a band approximately 32cm by 14cm in size.

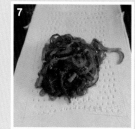

7. Prick with a fork then spread the onion jam in the centre, leaving a 2cm edge all round.

8. Sprinkle on the cheese topped by the anchovies and olives.

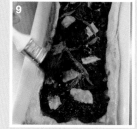

9. Bake at 190C/Gas Mark 5 for 15 minutes until the edges are risen and golden then brush the tart with olive oil.

Place in a suitable dish and serve immediately.

If some of your guests are vegetarian, you can simply leave out the anchovies for a veggie version.

I adore lamb in whatever style it's served. This recipe is a top-notch, restaurant-style dish, which is very simple to prepare, but the end result is fit for serving to everyone from close family members to your boss. It's a great way to use new season lamb.

Ingredients

Serves four

2 racks of lamb (ask your butcher to "French trim" this for you then brown the bones with some vegetables and tomato purée to make a reduced stock)

125ml lamb stock

100g fresh, white breadcrumbs

100g black olives

100g seed mustard

1 large bunch parsley, chopped

800g vegetables: red, green and yellow peppers, aubergine, onion, courgette and ripe tomatoes

50g butter

Splash sweet sherry, Madeira or port

Splash olive oil

Step by step

1 Chop the assorted vegetables.

2 Tear off the fat and skin from the lamb.

3 Heat the olive oil then seal the meat on both sides.

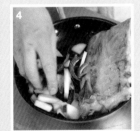
4 Add the vegetables to the pan then roast for 10 minutes at 200C/Gas Mark 6.

5 Remove the lamb from the oven then brush the back generously with the mustard.

6 Pat on a 50/50 mixture of breadcrumbs and parsley then drizzle the meat with melted butter.

7 Cook for another five minutes or, if you prefer your meat well done, 10 minutes, then remove the lamb and the vegetables.

8 **Make the sauce:** Put the sherry into the roasting pan.

9 Add the lamb stock and a knob of butter then stir well.

10 Carve the meat between each bone, place the vegetables on a plate with the lamb on top and add some sauce.

This roast is ideal for two (simply halve the ingredients) or even just for one if you're feeling hungry.

If you have one of those saucepans which transfers from the hob to the oven then that's the pan to use when making this dish. If not, simply transfer the meat into a roasting dish. The lamb goes well with the broccoli and anchovy butter, the olive capanata or simply some couscous.

Ingredients

Serves four

4 lamb rumps
2 red onions
Few sprigs rosemary, fresh mint and thyme
3 cloves garlic
1 dessertspoon balsamic vinegar
1 dessertspoon olive oil
Salt and pepper

Step by step

Rub the lamb with some of the rosemary.

Chop the mint and thyme.

Peel the red onions and cut them into quarters.

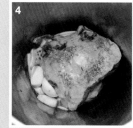

Place the meat in a bowl with the rosemary, mint, thyme, olive oil and garlic and mix well.

Remove the garlic from the marinade then place the lamb and herb mixture into the pan.

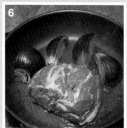

Add the onions.

Add the rest of the rosemary.

Place the mixture in the oven at 200C/Gas Mark 6 for 15 minutes.

Remove the pan from the oven, pour the vinegar into the pan and swirl it round to mix it with the juices.

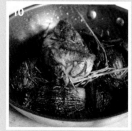

Allow the meat to rest for 10 minutes before carving.

If you can leave the lamb marinating in the herbs, garlic and oil overnight it will taste even better.

Mutton has come back into fashion again, perhaps partly because it's cheaper than lamb. Dameon Last keeps rare breed Norfolk Longhorns at Salhouse and apparently he has one of the only flocks of these animals used commercially for mutton; we get our mutton from him.

Ingredients

Serves four (freezable)

For the meatballs

450g minced mutton
2 cloves garlic
Few leaves fresh oregano
1 dessertspoon grated Parmesan
2 slices white bread
1 dessertspoon olive oil
Salt and pepper

For the spaghetti and tomato sauce

200g spaghetti
1 large tin chopped tomatoes
1 onion
1 clove garlic
1 tablespoon olive oil
Handful fresh parsley

Step by step

Dice the garlic, chop the oregano and add these to the minced mutton.

Add the grated Parmesan cheese.

Season liberally with salt and pepper.

Add the breadcrumbs.

Add the olive oil.

Use the palms of your hands to shape the mixture into little balls.

Make the tomato sauce: Slice the onion and chop the garlic then fry these together.

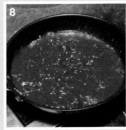
Add the tomatoes to the onion and garlic then warm through.

Cook the spaghetti then stir in the chopped parsley.

Place the meatballs in the sauce then cook on the hob or in the oven at 200C/Gas Mark 6 for 20 minutes. Serve with the spaghetti.

If you can't get mutton, use minced lamb instead. You could also swap the tomato sauce for capanata.

Vegetarian main courses

These days catering for vegetarians is a large part of our business. Vegetarian food has come a long way in recent years, and often the vegetarian dishes are so appealing that meat-eaters will choose to order them anyway. My eldest daughter Alison has been a vegetarian for years and she's a good sounding board; there are dishes, such as the summer vegetable pudding, which are often on our menus as they're among Alison's favourites and, of course, because they've proved popular with our other vegetarian guests.

This is a great dish as it's a world away from those pasta bakes and stir-fries that vegetarians often seem to live on. It's nice to have a change and this popular pie is an unusual take on the regular, meat-based Shepherd's pie. It is still a wonderful winter warmer...just without the meat.

Ingredients

Serves four (freezable)

1kg parsnips, peeled and cored
450g green lentils
150g Binham or Shropshire Blue
150g butter
1 large onion
1 Bramley apple
4 ripe tomatoes
400ml vegetable stock
2 teaspoons grain mustard
Few sprigs parsley

Step by step

1 Rinse the lentils then bring them to the boil with the stock. Simmer until cooked, adding more water as required.

2 Bring the parsnips to the boil and simmer until soft.

3 Dice the onion then peel and chop the apple. Simmer these in half the butter.

4 Peel, de-seed and chop the tomatoes (blanch them for a few seconds first).

5 Add the tomatoes to the softened onion and apple mixture.

6 Add the lentils and stir in the mustard.

7 Place the parsnips in a food processor, season well then add the remaining butter.

8 Place the lentil mix into an ovenproof dish then pipe the parsnip purée on top.

9 Top with the cheese.

10 Bake the dish for 30 minutes at 190C/Gas Mark 5 until piping hot and golden brown.

Unlike potatoes, you can purée parsnips in a food processor without them becoming sticky.

This is a real treat for the vegetarian in the family - you can make dainty, individual puddings for a starter or create more substantial ones, with extra goat's cheese, for a main course. They can be served cold, or warm if you prefer, if the sun's disappeared by the time you're ready to eat.

Ingredients

Makes four individual puddings

600g vegetables: aubergine, courgette, red onion, mixed peppers, ripe tomatoes and celery
1 small loaf sun-dried tomato bread
100g goat's cheese
12 pitted, large black olives
1 dessertspoon extra virgin olive oil
1 dessertspoon balsamic vinegar
100ml good quality tomato juice
Few sprigs fresh thyme
2 to 3 drops Tabasco
Handful salad leaves

Step by step

1 Put the tomato juice, Tabasco and olive oil in a bowl.

2 Cut the bread into thin slices.

3 Line the pudding basins with clingfilm, leaving some around the top.

4 Dip the bread into the tomato juice mixture and line the basins, overlapping the edges slightly.

5 Dice the aubergine, courgette, red onion, peppers, tomatoes, celery and thyme then fry these in olive oil.

6 Add the balsamic vinegar and a spoonful of the tomato mixture and continue to fry.

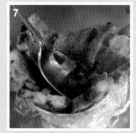
7 Place the vegetables into the lined basins.

8 Place some goat's cheese and a few olives into the centre of each of the puddings.

9 Add more filling and top with bread then wrap the clingfilm around the top of the puddings.

Place a saucer on top of each pudding to weigh it down then chill for two hours. Turn out and dress with salad leaves.

If you like to ring the changes, you can use beetroot or carrot juice instead of tomato juice.

In the autumn we get lots of different types of squash and often these are donated by customers. The squash ranges from huge pumpkins to little patty pans and they can all be adapted for this recipe. Use whatever you can find in the farm shops or, even better, grow your own!

Ingredients

Serves four

1 large butternut squash
2 large carrots
Two sprigs marjoram
1 teaspoon crushed peppercorns
1 tomato
1 dessertspoon low-fat cream cheese
Splash lemon juice

Step by step

1 Peel the butternut squash and cut it into four large chunks then hollow out the insides with a spoon.

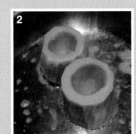

2 Melt some butter in a pan and fry the chunks of squash for a few minutes.

3 Transfer the squash to the oven and bake at 180C/Gas Mark 4 for 10 minutes.

4 Wash and grate the carrots.

5 Add the marjoram to the grated carrot along with the crushed black peppercorns.

6 Cut the tomato into quarters, remove the flesh then chop into small pieces.

7 Add the tomato to the carrot mixture.

8 Add the lemon juice and stir in the cream cheese.

9 Take the squash out of the oven and fill it with the carrot mixture then return it to the oven for 10 minutes.

10 Place on a plate and decorate with marjoram.

Remove the flesh from the tomato before chopping it as otherwise the mixture will be too watery.

This makes one large frittata or four small individual ones. Traditionally it's served hot but it can also be served cold, for a picnic, for example. The duck's eggs lend this a slightly different flavour from normal ones but you can use large hen's eggs, too. We use free-range eggs.

Ingredients

Serves four

8 duck's eggs or 6 hen's eggs
450g potatoes
125g butter
100g feta cheese
Handful cherry tomatoes
2 large onions
1 courgette
2 large cloves garlic
1 dessertspoon olive oil
Pinch salt
Milled black pepper

Step by step

1 Dice the potatoes then simmer them until they're just cooked.

2 Slice the onions.

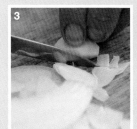

3 Chop the garlic.

4 Heat the olive oil then fry the onions and garlic until soft.

5 Peel and dice the courgette and add this to the onion mixture.

6 Add the diced potatoes to the courgette and onion mixture.

7 Break the duck's eggs into a bowl with the salt and black pepper and whisk together.

8 Pour in the eggs.

9 Place the cubed feta cheese and tomatoes on top.

10 Place the pan in the oven at 190C/Gas Mark 5 or put it on the hob until the eggs have set (around 10 minutes).

If you're a meat-eater, trying adding some chorizo to this - the oil will add flavour as it cooks.

This is a fabulous French dish. We make a lot of choux pastry and if we have any left over we use it for savoury éclairs or for fritters such as the red pepper and courgette ones pictured later on in this section. You can use button mushrooms, but wild ones will add texture and flavour.

Ingredients

Serves four

For the choux pastry

45g plain flour
30g butter
75ml water
25g Parmesan cheese
2 small eggs
Pinch salt

For the filling

1kg wild mushrooms
100ml tomato juice
Splash sweet sherry
1 onion
Pinch salt

Step by step

Make the pastry: Put the water and butter into a saucepan and bring this up to the boil.

Remove from the heat, add the flour and mix well.

Return to the heat and cook until the mixture leaves the sides of the pan, stirring often.

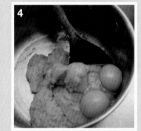

Leave the mixture to cool slightly. Grate the Parmesan then beat the cheese into the mixture with the eggs.

Make the filling: Chop the onion and the mushrooms then soften them in a frying pan.

Add the sweet sherry.

Add the tomato juice and salt and return to the heat.

Spoon the mushroom mixture into an ovenproof dish.

Place the pastry mixture into a piping bag and pipe it around the edge of the dish.

Bake at 200C/Gas Mark 6 for 12 minutes.

I used ceps, Paris brown, and yellow and green oyster mushrooms, but just use what's available.

This popular vegetarian dish works well as a main course or a starter. You can speed things up by making the cakes a couple of days before you need them then frying them when you're ready. Meanwhile, the coriander, chilli and red pepper salsa gives this some extra zing.

Ingredients

Makes 12

400g cooked chickpeas
2 small red chillies
100ml Greek yoghurt
15g fresh coriander
1 heaped teaspoon coriander seeds
1 heaped teaspoon cumin seeds
50g butter
1 small onion
1 small green pepper
3 large garlic cloves
1 teaspoon turmeric
Zest and juice of ½ lemon
Salt and black pepper

For frying
2 tablespoons groundnut oil

For the salsa
Small bunch coriander
¼ red pepper
½ small red chilli
Juice and zest of ½ lemon
Pinch sea salt

Step by step

1 Pulse the chickpeas in a food processor, leaving them slightly coarse.

2 Crush the cumin and coriander seeds and add these and the turmeric to the chickpeas.

3 Add the chopped coriander and yoghurt then season with salt and pepper.

4 Dice the onion, green pepper, garlic and chilli and mix well.

5 Fry these in the butter.

6 Add the fried onion mix to the chickpea mixture.

7 Mix well.

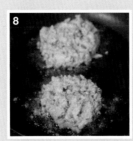

8 Heat the groundnut oil then fry ladles of the mixture for a few minutes on each side.

9 **Make the salsa:** Chop the coriander, red pepper and chilli then add the lemon juice and sea salt.

Place the cakes on the plates then top them with the salsa.

If you're counting calories, you can bake these chickpea cakes rather than fry them if you wish.

This is an upmarket take on cauliflower cheese. It makes a great side dish or can be turned into a quick and easy main course. I've used St Peter's Golden Ale here which comes from St Peter's Brewery in South Elmham in Suffolk, but Woodforde's Wherry also works well.

Ingredients

Serves four

1 large cauliflower
100g walnuts
200g blue cheese
2 large sticks celery
200ml whipping cream
100ml bitter
½ onion
1 teaspoon chopped chives

Step by step

Wash the cauliflower and break it into florets.

Place the florets in a pan of water, bring to the boil and simmer for four minutes. Strain and place on one side.

Finely slice the onion.

Chop the celery.

Put the onion and celery in a saucepan.

Pour in the beer then add the cream.

Bring to the boil and simmer until the mixture has reduced by half (around five minutes).

Take the mixture off the boil and stir in the cauliflower florets.

Crumble in half the cheese then return to the heat to warm through.

Place into a serving dish and crumble the rest of the cheese on top. Sprinkle on some walnuts and decorate with chopped chives.

This makes a really quick supper dish and can also be used as an accompaniment to pork dishes.

These are very popular at The Pigs pub in Edgefield. They're similar to fish cakes, but the crushed new potatoes rather than mashed potato make them more substantial. You can use English onions but using a number of different varieties makes them more interesting.

Ingredients

Serves four

For the potato cakes

1 small white onion
1 small red onion
4 spring onions
1 leek
Good bunch chives
450g new potatoes
100g strong Cheddar or Lancashire cheese
1 egg
1 dessertspoon olive oil
Black pepper
50g butter
150g white breadcrumbs

For the chutney

2 Bramley apples
1 dessertspoon white wine vinegar
1 dessertspoon granulated sugar
½ white onion
2 dessertspoons water

Step by step

1 Leave the skin on the new potatoes and cut them in half. Place them in a saucepan of water and bring it to the boil.

2 Finely dice the leek, chives, spring onions and red onion and mix these together.

3 Chop the white onion for the potato cakes and the half white onion for the chutney then set a third of this aside.

4 Stir the chopped onion into the leek, chive, spring onion and red onion mixture.

5 Once cooked, drain the potatoes and crush them in the pan. Add the olive oil.

6 Season the potatoes with black pepper and add the fresh thyme.

7 Mix the onions with the potatoes.

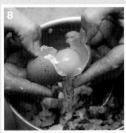

8 Crumble the cheese into the onion and potato mixture and add the egg and the breadcrumbs. Mix well.

9 Make the chutney: Fry the onion then add the apples and the water. Cook on a low heat until the fruit reduces to a purée.

10 Fry spoonfuls of the mixture in butter for three minutes on each side. Place on plates, spoon on the chutney and decorate with chives.

These potato cakes are quite soft so remember to take care when lifting them out of the pan.

Olive capanata

Capanata is an aubergine stew, a little bit like ratatouille, and is a quick and easy dish to make. Grill some bread to go with it (we make our own at The Lavender House) and then brush it with olive oil. Rustic, country bread such as focaccia or fresh olive bread will go well with this.

Ingredients
Serves four

100g best quality mixed marinated olives
1 x 400g tin chopped tomatoes
1 large aubergine
1 onion
2 cloves garlic
Few leaves fresh oregano
Few leaves fresh mint
100ml olive oil
Bread to serve (see above)

Step by step

Finely dice the onion.

Chop the garlic.

Trim, slice then dice the aubergine.

Fry the onion in the olive oil until soft.

Stir in the aubergine.

Add the chopped tomatoes.

Stir in the olives.

Chop the mint and oregano and mix this in.

Slice the bread and brush it on both sides with olive oil.

Grill the slices of bread for a few minutes then top it with the capanata mixture.

You can use capanata in pasta dishes, as a pizza topping or even serve it on its own as a salad.

These fritters are truly delicious when they're served piping hot straight from the deep fat fryer so try to eat them immediately if you can. They go well with the salsa featured with the chilli, chickpea and coriander cakes, and you can make smaller ones as party nibbles.

Ingredients

Serves four

½ red pepper
1 large courgette
45g plain flour
30g butter
75ml water
25g Parmesan cheese
1 small red chilli
2 spring onions
2 small eggs
Good pinch rock salt
Vegetable oil for frying

Step by step

1. Put the water and butter into a saucepan and bring this up to the boil.

2. Remove the pan from the heat, add the flour and mix well.

3. Return to the heat and cook until the mixture leaves the sides of the pan, stirring often.

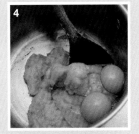

4. Leave the mixture to cool slightly. Grate the Parmesan then beat this into the mixture along with the eggs.

5. Peel and dice the courgette and wash and dice the red pepper.

6. Finely dice the chilli.

7. Mix the vegetables with the choux pastry mixture and stir until combined.

8. Finely chop the spring onions and add these to the mixture.

9. Mould the mixture into small balls then place these into a deep fat fryer for around four minutes.

10. Drain the fritters on greaseproof paper and place on a serving dish. Decorate with the spring onion tops then sprinkle with rock salt.

Don't worry if you're not a fan of spicy food - just leave out the chilli then make these the same way.

Side dishes

There are so many delicious side dishes to choose from that it was difficult to decide what to select for this book. In the end I opted for recipes that are a little out of the ordinary but which are still very easy to do - that way you can jazz up a roast or a family meal with a few seasonal vegetables. Visiting farm shops or farmers' markets for vegetables is all the rage these days but they've become fashionable again for a reason - at HFG farmshops, which are the ones we use most, they have such a wide variety of fresh produce that it's hard to know what not to buy!

Mrs Temple's Binham Blue is a lovely cheese which comes from Wighton near Wells in North Norfolk and which can be found in delis all over the county. Thanks to the Binham Blue, this dish is nice and creamy and, because of the apples, it goes particularly well with roast pork.

Ingredients

Serves four

50g Binham Blue
2 large leeks
1 Bramley apple
125ml whipping cream
50g butter
Salt and freshly milled black pepper

Step by step

1. Wash and finely slice the leeks.

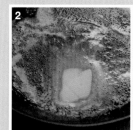

2. Melt the butter in a frying pan.

3. Add the chopped leeks and fry gently.

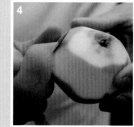

4. Peel and slice the apple.

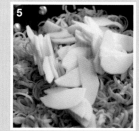

5. Add the apple to the leek and continue to fry until soft.

6. Season well.

7. Take the mixture off the hob then pour in the cream.

8. Return the pan to the hob and bring the mixture to the boil.

9. Place the leek mixture in an ovenproof dish then crumble the cheese on top.

Place under the grill or in the oven at 200C/Gas Mark 6 until the cheese is golden brown.

If you can't get hold of Binham Blue you can always use Stilton or Roquefort for this dish.

This is a real comfort dish that goes perfectly with a Sunday roast. Use a mandolin to slice the potatoes if you've got one as the thinner the slices, the quicker the cooking time. Maris Piper potatoes work well for this and you can also use Gruyère cheese if you prefer.

Ingredients

Serves four

1kg potatoes
250ml single cream
100g Norfolk Alpine cheese
1 clove garlic
Salt and freshly ground black pepper
Few sprigs parsley to garnish

Step by step

Slice the garlic and place this in a pan with the cream.

Bring the cream and garlic to the boil.

Peel the potatoes then slice them finely.

Season these liberally with salt and pepper.

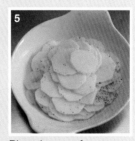

Place layers of the potatoes in an ovenproof dish.

Finely grate the cheese.

Place the cheese on top of the potatoes.

Ladle the cream on top.

Put the dish in the oven at 160C/Gas Mark 3 for 90 minutes.

Decorate the dish with parsley before serving.

You can make up portions of this for individual side dishes if you like or simply opt for one large dish.

To make this a little different you can add some wild or button mushrooms or some diced celery or fennel to the mix. And if you haven't got much time, you can speed things up by leaving out the walnut and parsley topping and simply baking the ratatouille with the goat's cheese.

Ingredients

Serves four

1 large Spanish onion
4 slices goat's cheese
1 yellow pepper
1 green pepper
1 red pepper
1 large courgette
1 large clove garlic
1 small tin chopped plum tomatoes
1 dessertspoon chopped walnuts
1 dessertspoon chopped parsley
1 dessertspoon white breadcrumbs
Handful mixed salad leaves
Salt and pepper

Step by step

Slice the onion.

Slice the peppers and dice the courgette.

Fry until soft.

Add the tomatoes and season well then fry for a few more minutes.

Tear the basil leaves and add these to the onion mixture.

Spoon the mixture into pastry cutters placed on a baking tray.

Place a piece of goat's cheese on top of each cutter.

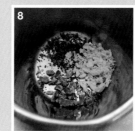

Mix together the walnuts, parsley and breadcrumbs.

Place the walnut mixture on top of the goat's cheese.

Place the dish in the oven at 200C/Gas Mark 6 until golden (around 15 minutes) then dress with the salad leaves.

This is a favourite starter at our bistro-style restaurant, Anna Sewell House, in Great Yarmouth.

This dish is like a stir-fry and so goes well with any poultry dish such as chicken or duck. We used to make this with those big, white Dutch cabbages but Hispy cabbage works just as well. It's best to use freshly grated nutmeg as it gives it more flavour than dried.

Ingredients

Serves four

1 large cabbage
2 rashers streaky bacon
25g pinenuts
¼ nutmeg
Salt and black pepper

Step by step

Trim and dice the bacon.

Slice the cabbage.

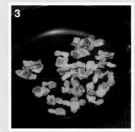

Fry the bacon in a dry pan.

Add the pinenuts.

Fry for a few more minutes, stirring occasionally.

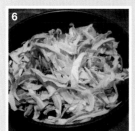

Add the cabbage.

Continue to fry the mixture, stirring well.

Grate the nutmeg over the cabbage (you need to season it well).

Season with salt and black pepper.

Pile on to a serving dish and decorate with a tiny sprinkle of nutmeg.

Just use a dry pan for this (ie. with no fat) as the fat from the bacon will cook the dish.

Once you're used to making this risotto, you can vary it with lots of other ingredients. This particular dish is ideal if you're watching your weight as it's nice and light. However, if you want to make it richer, you can finish it off by stirring in some cream and Parmesan cheese.

Ingredients

Serves four (freezable)

125g Arborio rice
250ml vegetable stock
100g frozen peas
100g broad beans
Few leaves fresh mint
4 spring onions
1 glass white wine
1 large leek
50g butter

Step by step

1 Finely chop the leek.

2 Put the butter and olive oil in a frying pan, add the onion and fry until soft.

3 Add the rice and cook for three minutes.

4 Make up the stock and add this to the pan a little at a time.

5 Continue adding the stock a little at a time, stirring continuously.

6 Finely chop the spring onions.

7 Add the peas, broad beans and spring onion to the pan.

8 Take off the heat, add the wine then return to the heat for two to three minutes.

9 Chop the mint and add to the mixture.

Pile the mixture into attractive dishes.

This dish is also ideal for meat-eaters: simply stir in a little ham or cooked chicken.

If you don't have baby onions you can used some sliced onion for this but the baby ones do look great. This dish goes very well with fish, and as it's popular on menus in France it always makes me think of sunny lunchtimes spent eating outside in French bistros – if only!

Ingredients

Serves four

200g frozen peas
1 baby gem lettuce
125g peeled silver skin onions
75ml white wine
75ml whipping cream
Few leaves fresh mint

Step by step

Put the wine into a pan.

Add the onions and bring up to the boil.

Add the peas.

Cut the lettuce into quarters.

Add the lettuce to the pan.

Pour in the cream, bring to the boil then reduce for two to three minutes.

Chop the mint.

Stir the mint into the mixture and heat through.

Season with salt and pepper.

Spoon into an attractive serving dish.

If you use petits pois rather than regular peas for this dish it'll look even more attractive.

This is a popular dish throughout South Asia and is very cheap to make. You can use a green pepper but a red one works better as it adds some colour and looks great. The dhal isn't particularly hot and thanks to the green apple it is slightly tart. It is delicious served hot or cold.

Ingredients

Serves four (freezable)

225g split red lentils
500ml water
1 teaspoon ground ginger
1 teaspoon ground cumin
1 teaspoon turmeric
1 teaspoon salt
1 teaspoon Madras curry powder
2 tablespoons butter
2 potatoes
1 large onion
1 clove garlic
1 small red pepper
1 small can chopped tomatoes
1 green apple
Few leaves coriander

Step by step

1 Put the water in a pan and add the turmeric, ginger, cumin and salt.

2 Bring the liquid up to the boil and stir in the lentils.

3 Dice the potatoes and add to the lentil mixture. Simmer for 20 minutes until the potatoes are nearly cooked.

4 Dice the red pepper and slice the onion then fry until soft.

5 Finely chop the garlic and add this to the pepper and onion.

6 Stir in the curry powder.

7 Add the chopped tomatoes.

8 Stir the pepper, onion and tomato mixture into the lentils then simmer for 10 minutes.

9 Grate the apple. Take the mixture off the heat and stir in the apple.

Spoon into attractive dishes and decorate with coriander.

The dhal can be served on its own as a dip or as a vegetable accompaniment to any spicy dish.

This makes a great accompaniment to lentil dhal or any spicy dish. Thanks to the star anise, cinnamon and other spices, the rice has a lovely colour and all kinds of different flavours. The result is a world away from the ready-prepared Pilau rice that you can buy in supermarkets.

Ingredients

Serves four

250g long grain rice
120g cashew nuts
3 tablespoons olive oil
4 cloves
1 star anise
2 cardamom pods
2cm piece cinnamon stick
1 teaspoon cumin seeds
6 shallots
120g raisins
1 teaspoon turmeric powder
500ml water
Pinch salt

Step by step

1. Place the cloves, cardamom, cinnamon, cumin seeds and star anise into a saucepan.

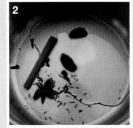

2. Add the olive oil.

3. Add the cashew nuts and fry for a few minutes.

4. Peel and dice the shallots.

5. Add these to the pan and continue to fry until soft.

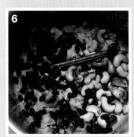

6. Add the raisins.

7. And the turmeric and salt and mix well.

8. Stir in the rice then cook for three minutes, stirring frequently.

9. Add the water and mix well.

10. Cover and cook until the water has been absorbed (around 20 minutes) then spoon into a serving dish.

Leave the cinnamon and star anise in when you serve it; no one will eat it but it looks very attractive.

This is a beautiful autumn dish which looks great because of its unusual colour. As it's quite sweet, it goes well with strong, fatty flavours such as duck or roast lamb. You can also make this with pumpkin which works well if you're planning a get-together for Hallowe'en.

Ingredients

Serves four

1 large butternut squash
1 dessertspoon honey
1 large piece root ginger
Knob butter
Handful pumpkin seeds

Step by step

Peel the butternut squash.

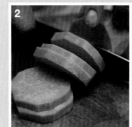

Slice the squash.

Put the squash in a pan of water and boil until tender (around five minutes).

Dice the ginger.

Melt the butter and add the honey.

Add the ginger.

Strain the squash and add the slices to the honey and ginger.

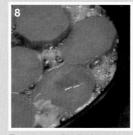

Return to the hob to warm through.

Sprinkle over the pumpkin seeds.

Spoon into an attractive serving dish.

If you make plenty you can turn this into a delicious soup by liquidising with some vegetable stock.

We use this recipe when we visit playgroups to teach them about good food – all the toddlers add their favourite vegetables and have a stir! If you like your food hot, you can make it spicier still by adding some ginger, coriander, cinnamon or curry powder.

Ingredients

Serves four (freezable)

⅓ red, yellow and green pepper
4 spring onions
2 carrots
Juice of 1 lemon
Zest of ½ lemon
½ teaspoon salt
1 teaspoon fennel seeds
125g dried couscous
250ml water or vegetable stock

Step by step

Slice the peppers.

Slice the spring onion.

Grate the carrot.

Peel and chop the lemon zest.

Mix the peppers, spring onion, carrot and lemon zest together.

Squeeze the lemon juice and add to the mixture.

Add the fennel seeds and the salt.

Stir in the dried couscous.

Boil the water or make up the vegetable stock and pour this in.

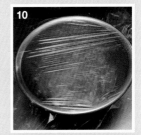

Cover the bowl with clingfilm and leave to stand for 15 minutes.

This makes a great picnic salad - you can add whatever takes your fancy from your fridge or garden.

We serve this with steak at The Pigs pub in Edgefield and it works very well. You can also dish it up with burgers, sausages or chicken wings as it makes an excellent accompaniment to barbecues. Alternatively, leave it to cool and serve it as a salad in its own right.

Ingredients

Serves four

400g cherry tomatoes
1 small red chilli or 1 medium chilli
1 onion
1 clove garlic
1 dessertspoon granulated sugar
1 dessertspoon tomato purée
1 dessertspoon white wine vinegar
1 dessertspoon olive oil
2 dessertspoons water

Step by step

1. Dice the onion.

2. Dice the red pepper and the chilli.

3. Slice the garlic.

4. Fry the onion, pepper, chilli and garlic in the olive oil.

5. Cut half the tomatoes in half and leave the rest whole.

6. Add the tomatoes to the pan.

7. Add the sugar and tomato purée.

8. Add the vinegar and the water.

9. Simmer on a very low heat for half an hour, stirring occasionally.

Take off the heat and leave to cool then serve in little jam jars or glass dishes.

If you have any chutney left over it'll keep for a few weeks in a sterilised jam jar or Kilner jar.

This American dish is lovely served with ribs or chicken and goes well with all kinds of barbecue food. It can be served hot or cold, and if you want to ring the changes you can fold through chopped spring onion tops or chives to make it a little different or top with sour cream.

Ingredients

Serves four

400g cooked mixed beans
200g chopped tomatoes
2 rashers thickly-cut smoked bacon
1 medium onion
1 dessertspoon black treacle
2 cloves garlic
1 dessertspoon white wine vinegar
1 dessertspoon honey
½ teaspoon English mustard powder
Few sprigs flat-leaf parsley

Step by step

Finely chop the garlic.

Dice the onion and mix this with the garlic.

Chop the bacon into bite-sized chunks.

Fry the bacon in a dry pan until crispy.

Add the onion and the garlic.

Add the black treacle and the mustard.

Stir in the beans.

Add the vinegar and the honey.

Add the chopped tomatoes.

Cook the mixture until reduced (around 20 minutes) then chop the flat-leaf parsley and stir this through.

We often have this as posh beans on toast for supper at the end of a shift.

At The Lavender House we only serve asparagus when it's in season, from the beginning of May until almost the end of June. Fresh Norfolk asparagus springs up all over the place during this time and you'll find it on sale everywhere from farm shops to makeshift roadside stalls.

Ingredients

Serves four

1kg asparagus

3 egg yolks

250g butter

1 dessertspoon white wine vinegar

2 dessertspoons tarragon

Step by step

1 Break off the woody parts of the asparagus at the base by bending each piece until it snaps and breaks.

2 Trim the base of each piece with a sharp knife.

3 Put some water on to boil then cook the asparagus for three minutes.

4 **Make the cheat's béarnaise:** Melt the butter gently in a saucepan.

5 Place the egg yolks in a food processor.

6 Add the white wine vinegar then blend the mixture for a few minutes until it is almost white.

7 Chop the tarragon.

8 With the machine on full speed, slowly add the melted butter to the mixture, followed by the chopped tarragon.

9 Drain the asparagus and place it on the plates.

10 Pour over the béarnaise and serve immediately.

Once the asparagus has been prepared, this is a very straightforward yet impressive spring dish.

This colourful side dish is a variation of the popular tomato and mozzarella salad but the difference is that it's baked. It looks great thanks to the contrasting colours, and taking the peel off the courgette makes it look more attractive. It makes a great summer starter, too.

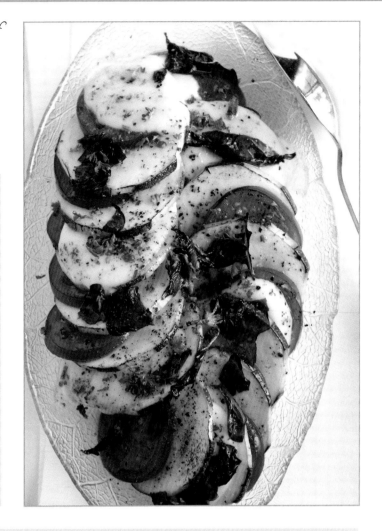

Ingredients

Serves four

1 large courgette
4 ripe tomatoes
125g mozzarella
50ml olive oil
Few basil leaves
Rock salt
Black pepper
Few sprigs parsley

Step by step

Remove some of the peel from the courgette.

Slice the courgette.

Slice the tomatoes.

Slice the mozzarella.

Arrange the courgette and tomato slices in an ovenproof dish.

Add the mozzarella.

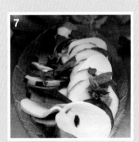

Tear the basil leaves and place these on top.

Sprinkle with salt and black pepper.

Pour over the olive oil.

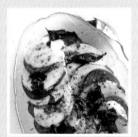

Place in the oven at 180C/Gas Mark 4 for 20 minutes then decorate with chopped parsley and a little more oil.

Try to use tomatoes that are nice and ripe as they'll make all the difference to the flavour.

This dish makes a tasty vegetarian starter in its own right and goes well with pork. Once they've been boiled, English onions are quite mild, and once baked they have a rather sweet taste which complements the Stilton nicely. If you're not a blue cheese fan, use goat's cheese instead.

Ingredients

Serves four

4 English onions
250g baby leaf spinach
100g Stilton
25g butter
Good pinch nutmeg
Salt and freshly ground black pepper

Step by step

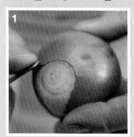

Peel the onions.

Simmer the onions for five minutes in boiling water.

Remove the middle of each onion with a sharp knife.

Chop up the middle sections.

Fry the middle sections in the butter.

Add the baby spinach and continue to fry.

Add the nutmeg then season with salt and pepper.

Take off the heat and crumble in the Stilton.

Place the onions in an ovenproof dish and stuff them with the cheese and spinach mixture.

Bake them in the oven at 180C/Gas Mark 4 until the cheese bubbles (around 20 minutes).

If you're not a fan of spinach you can always use mushrooms instead, either wild or button ones.

Sprouting broccoli is in season in early spring and goes really well with this salty, fishy butter. You can also use normal broccoli for this or curly kale or cabbage in winter. I like to serve this with skate but you can also serve it with herrings, trout or other oily fish.

Ingredients

Serves four

500g broccoli (prepared weight)
125g butter
Four large anchovy fillets
Large handful fresh parsley
Juice of ½ lemon
½ teaspoon smoked paprika

Step by step

Soften the butter in the microwave.

Add the lemon juice to the butter.

Chop the anchovies and add them to the butter.

Finely chop the parsley.

Add the parsley to the butter mixture and mix well.

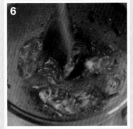

Stir in the paprika then place the butter mixture in the fridge.

Trim the broccoli stalks.

Place these in a pan of boiling water and cook until tender (around five minutes).

Place the broccoli on a serving dish and take the butter out of the fridge.

Spoon the anchovy butter over the broccoli and serve.

I love this as a little starter - it's very unusual but has really vibrant flavours!

Anya potatoes look very exotic but in fact they're grown on my home turf, the flat fields of the Fens. You can, of course, use Jersey Royals or pink fir potatoes for this dish instead, or, better still, potatoes that you've grown in your own garden or allotment; nothing's better than those!

Ingredients

Serves four

1kg Anya potatoes
50g whole hazelnuts
100g butter
Small bunch sage
Salt and freshly ground black pepper

Step by step

1. Put the potatoes on to boil.

2. Toast the hazelnuts in a hot oven for two to three minutes.

3. Rub the hazelnuts between your palms to remove the skin.

4. Break the nuts up with a rolling pin.

5. Heat most of the butter in a frying pan.

6. Fry the potatoes until golden.

7. Season with salt and pepper.

8. Tear the sage and add this to the potatoes, saving a few leaves for decoration.

9. Fry the potatoes for a few more minutes then spoon them into a serving dish.

Add some more butter to the pan, swirl round then pour this over the top of the potatoes. Decorate with the remaining sage leaves.

If you have any uncooked potatoes left over they should keep at room temperature for up to two weeks.

Coating the parsnips in flour before roasting them makes them nice and crispy on the outside, while the hot oven turns the insides fluffy and soft – what more could you ask from your vegetables?!
A real winter dish, these tasty parsnips go really well with all manner of roasts.

Ingredients

Serves four

4 large parsnips
2 dessertspoons plain flour
1 dessertspoon English mustard powder
1 dessertspoon olive oil
50g butter

Step by step

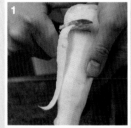

Peel the parsnips.

Cut each parsnip into quarters.

Place them in boiling water and bring back up to the boil.

Simmer for five minutes until just cooked.

Sieve the flour and mustard powder together.

In a hot oven, melt the olive oil and butter together on a baking tray.

Drain the parsnips.

Toss them in the flour and mustard powder.

Put them on a baking tray.

Place them in the oven at 200C/Gas Mark 6, for around 15 minutes, turning occasionally.

Next time you roast potatoes, try coating them in flour, too, to ensure that they're really crispy.

The turmeric in this dish gives it some colour and the sparkling water makes it a little lighter than usual (you can use normal water if you haven't got sparkling). You can also swap the turmeric for paprika, cayenne pepper or mustard powder if you like your food on the hot side.

Ingredients

Serves four

1 large cauliflower
2 dessertspoons cornflour
Large pinch salt
1 pinch turmeric
125ml sparkling water
125g plain flour
Vegetable oil for deep frying

Step by step

Trim the cauliflower and break off the florets.

Place these in a pan of water and bring them to the boil.

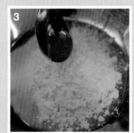

Make the tempura batter: Place the cornflour, salt and turmeric in a bowl.

Pour in the water and mix well.

Drain the cauliflower.

Lightly dust the florets with the cornflour.

Dip the cauliflower florets in the batter.

Heat the vegetable oil to 170C.

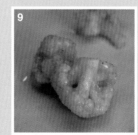

Fry the florets for two to three minutes until they're nicely coloured.

Drain the florets on greaseproof paper, place them in a serving dish then dust them with the turmeric.

You can also make fritters with courgettes or broccoli - just dip them in the batter and fry.

Fennel has a strong aniseed flavour and is very popular in Italian cookery. It can be eaten raw as it's crisp and full of flavour so works well in salads but when it's cooked it's softer and more mellow. It's available all year round, but is at its best from June to September.

Ingredients

Serves four

2 large fennel
½ onion
Zest and juice of 1 orange
Pinch fresh saffron threads
125ml water
Freshly ground black pepper

Step by step

Wash the fennel. Slice off the shoots and root, peel off the outer layer then cut the fennel into slices.

Set the fennel tops aside for decoration.

Slice the onion.

Put the fennel and onion slices into a deep pan.

Add the orange zest.

Pour in the orange juice.

Add the saffron then season with pepper.

Pour the water over the fennel and onion mixture.

Cover the pan and cook gently on the hob until the fennel is soft (around 15 minutes).

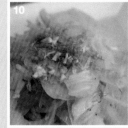

When the fennel is cooked, decorate it with the chopped fennel tops.

You can use a mandolin to cut the fennel into very thin slices but watch your fingers!

Desserts

Anyone who knows me well will know that I've got a very sweet tooth and like nothing better than chocolate, confectionery and ice cream. At The Lavender House I'm very fortunate to have a team of chefs who are all skilled in the art of dessert-making and consequently they create some truly wonderful concoctions. The trick with desserts is to make them as visually appealing as possible so that they create a wow factor before the guests even start to tuck in; hopefully the desserts on the following pages do just that. And if you go out to dinner, please don't deprive yourself – make sure you order a delicious dessert or two!

Once soft fruit is in season, get picking then you can transform your favourite berries into an ice cream treat that doesn't feature chocolate flakes or sugar cones. We have some fabulous ice cream producers in Norfolk but it's well worth making your own for special occasions.

Ingredients

Serves four

For the semi-freddo

225g raspberries
225g mascarpone
250ml whipping cream
5 egg yolks
5 tablespoons caster sugar
2 tablespoons orange juice

For the orange and ginger syrup

225g sugar
Juice of 2 oranges and zest of 1 orange
2 tablespoons whisky
25g fresh ginger, chopped
Juice of 1 lemon
50ml water

Step by step

Place all the syrup ingredients into a pan, bring to the boil and reduce by half then leave to cool.

Prepare the semi-freddo mixture:
Whisk the egg yolks and sugar over hot water until double in volume.

Add the mascarpone and continue whisking.

Add the orange juice and whisk again.

Whip the cream.

Fold this gently into the semi-freddo mixture.

Put the raspberries in a bowl and combine them with the syrup.

Spoon some raspberry mixture into the glasses followed by some cream then more raspberries.

Place in the freezer for 45 minutes.

Serve with little shortbread biscuits dusted with icing sugar.

This lovely dessert also works well with blackcurrants, blackberries and gooseberries.

What can be more luxurious than a jelly made with champagne? And with fresh, ripe berries this dessert is fit for a king. If you can't stretch to champers you can use Cava, Asti or Italian Prosecco instead; however, if it's for a celebration, why not treat yourself to the real thing?

Ingredients

Makes four large or eight small fruit jellies

37cl bottle of champagne (rosé works well)
250g assorted summer berries
125ml diluted summer fruit squash
125g caster sugar
3 leaves gelatine
Good sprig fresh mint

Step by step

1. Soak the gelatine in cold water.

2. Leave it for five minutes until soft then squeeze out the water.

3. Bring the diluted fruit squash to the boil then add the gelatine.

4. Whisk the mixture until the gelatine has completely dissolved.

5. Add the sugar and whisk until dissolved.

6. Pour the mixture into a bowl and allow to cool.

7. Place the fruit and mint leaves into chilled champagne glasses or glass bowls.

8. When the gelatine starts to set, add the well-chilled champagne.

9. Gently pour the champagne mixture into the glasses and top up as the bubbles settle.

10. Refrigerate for four hours until set.

Strawberries and raspberries are my favourites for this but blueberries and blackberries work well, too.

The beauty of this dish is that you can serve it as a fondant pudding with its own chocolate sauce, or cook it for a little longer and create a proper cake. Vary the presentation with ramekins, teacups or individual glass bowls, but remember to always use something microwaveable.

Ingredients

Serves four (freezable)

125g butter
80g cocoa powder
375g self-raising flour
½ teaspoon bicarbonate of soda
250g caster sugar
2 eggs
250ml water
1 tablespoon icing sugar

Step by step

Sieve the cocoa powder and flour together.

Stir in the bicarbonate of soda.

Put the butter, sugar and water into a bowl and microwave on full power for 90 seconds.

Add the cocoa mixture to the butter, sugar and water mixture.

Beat well.

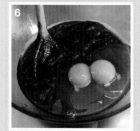

Break the eggs into the chocolate mixture.

Beat again.

Fill each ramekin three-quarters full and place these in the microwave.

Cook on full power for three to four minutes to make a soft pudding or for six to seven minutes to make a cake.

Turn the puddings out and decorate with icing sugar before serving.

Once you've mastered this dish, show off your culinary skills by whipping up a dessert in no time!

This dish is ideal during the winter months and at Christmas time can be served on the day itself as an alternative to Christmas pudding, or for Boxing Day tea. The walnuts lend it a festive flavour and it works well served warm with hot rum custard, or cold with clotted cream.

Ingredients

Makes a 20cm tart (freezable)

For the pastry

250g plain flour
140g butter
50g icing sugar
Zest of ½ lemon
1 egg yolk
Cold water to bind

For the filling

250g fresh breadcrumbs
250g black treacle
100ml whipping cream
50g chopped walnuts
Juice of 1 small lemon
1 egg

Step by step

Make the pastry: Blend all the pastry ingredients together in a food processor.

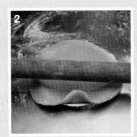

Line the flan tin with the pastry, leaving some above the rim.

Line the tin with greaseproof paper and baking beans then bake for 10 minutes at 180C/Gas Mark 4 until set.

Make the filling: Pour the black treacle into a bowl.

Add the lemon zest.

Add the lemon juice and the breadcrumbs.

Add the egg and the cream and stir well.

Add the walnuts.

Pour the treacle mixture into the pastry case.

Bake at 180C/Gas Mark 4 for 25 minutes. Allow the tart to cool before cutting and serving.

You can make this in advance to take the stress out of the big day, if you can resist eating it, that is!

Most cooks love the spring because of the lamb, asparagus and the first of the shellfish. But I particularly like the winter because of oxtail soup, plump pheasants, stew and dumplings and, of course, steaming hot puddings. After all, nobody makes a pud like the Brits!

Ingredients

Serves four (freezable)

For the pudding

175g dates simmered in 300ml water
175g muscavado sugar
175g plain flour
2 teaspoons baking powder
50g butter
2 eggs

For the sauce

300ml single cream
50g walnuts
50g muscavado sugar
1 dessertspoon black treacle

Step by step

1 Grease the pudding basin with butter.

2 Cream the butter and sugar together until light and fluffy.

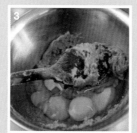

3 Add the eggs and beat the mixture well.

4 Add the flour and the baking powder.

5 Stone and chop the dates then add these to the mix.

6 Spoon the mixture into the pudding basin.

7 Cook at 180C/Gas Mark 4 for around 30 minutes.

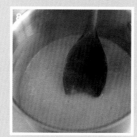

8 **Prepare the sauce:** First simmer the cream and sugar together for a few minutes.

9 Add the treacle. Chop the walnuts then mix these in. Bring to the boil then simmer for five minutes.

10 Turn the pudding out then pour the hot sauce over the top.

This gloriously sweet dish is the epitome of a winter dessert and works well with this simple sauce.

Everyone knows that chocolate is supposed to be an aphrodisiac, and these chocolate pancakes will surely melt the hardest of hearts. Serve them to the one you love on Valentine's Day, as a teatime treat for friends and family, or, better still, as a decadent breakfast in bed!

Ingredients

Makes 12 small pancakes

For the pancakes
250g plain flour
250ml milk
50g cocoa
50g melted butter
50g icing sugar
2 eggs
½ teaspoon baking powder

For the sauce
250ml water
125g strong cooking chocolate (at least 50% cocoa)
25g butter
25g cocoa powder
Few spoonfuls natural yoghurt
Few fresh mint leaves to decorate

Step by step

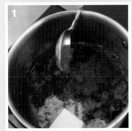

Make the sauce: Bring the water, butter, chocolate and cocoa powder to the boil, stirring continuously.

Make the pancakes: Sieve the cocoa, flour, icing sugar and baking powder into a bowl.

Break the eggs into the centre of the mixture and whisk until smooth.

Slowly add the milk.

Melt the butter in a pan then add a tablespoon of chocolate mixture for each pancake.

Cook for a couple of minutes on both sides.

Pile the pancakes on to an attractive plate.

Pour some of the chocolate sauce over the pancakes.

Place a spoonful of yoghurt on top.

Decorate with some fresh mint leaves.

Chocolate is the food of the gods and these delicious pancakes look and taste heavenly!

Apple charlotte

This dessert works well served warm with custard, or you can rustle up some simple butterscotch sauce to go with it by melting some butter and sugar together and adding a spoonful of double cream. On a hot day you can cool the dish down by adding some ice cream or clotted cream.

Ingredients
Makes four (freezable)

1kg Bramley apples
125g butter
125g sugar
12 slices white bread
Small pinch grated nutmeg
Juice of ½ lemon

Step by step

Peel, core and chop the Bramley apples.

Fry the apple pieces in the butter until soft.

Add the lemon juice and stir in the sugar, leaving a little aside.

Brush the ramekins with butter then coat them with sugar.

With a pastry cutter, cut out eight small rounds of bread.

Cut the rest of the bread into strips.

Put a bread disc at the bottom of each ramekin, line them with bread slices then sprinkle them with sugar.

Place spoonfuls of the apple mixture into each dish and top with another disc of bread.

Cover each ramekin with clingfilm then place a saucer on top for 15 minutes in order to weigh them down.

Remove the saucers and clingfilm then bake at 190C/Gas Mark 5 for 20 minutes until golden.

If you want to vary this dish simply add some cinnamon, dates, sultanas, raisins or prunes.

This is a Christmas dish and makes an interesting alternative to mince pies. You can either prepare one large strüdel or make smaller individual ones as I've done here. If you're feeling decadent, add some cognac to the mixture and serve the strüdels with ice cream or clotted cream.

Ingredients

Serves four (freezable)

200g mincemeat
125g butter
4 sheets filo pastry
2 dessertspoons icing sugar
1 dessert apple
25ml brandy

Step by step

1 Put the mincemeat into a bowl.

2 Peel, core and chop the apple.

3 Add the apple to the mincemeat.

4 Add the brandy to the apple and mincemeat mixture.

5 Melt the butter. Place the pastry sheets on a clean surface and brush them with melted butter.

6 Split the mincemeat mixture between the pastry sheets and roll them up carefully.

7 Place some butter on the edge of each strüdel then press the edges firmly together.

8 Coat the strüdels with butter and place them on a baking tray.

9 Sprinkle the strüdels with icing sugar.

Cook at 200C/Gas Mark 6 for 15 minutes then dust with icing sugar again before serving.

To make these even more festive, add a little cinnamon or even mix in some cranberry sauce.

Baked croissant pudding

This dish is a different take on classic bread and butter pudding although it's a little richer than the traditional version. It's perfect for serving to friends and family during the holidays and ideal for warming you up after a bracing walk along the beach or through the countryside.

Ingredients

Serves four

5 croissants
2 eggs
2 egg yolks
60g butter
250ml single cream
100g raisins
50g caster sugar
½ teaspoon cinnamon
½ vanilla pod
Dash Grand Marnier, Amaretto or cherry brandy (optional)
Sprinkle icing sugar
3 dessertspoons apricot jam

Step by step

1 Halve the croissants and butter generously.

2 Simmer the raisins in a little water for five minutes.

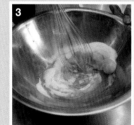

3 Whisk the egg yolks with the sugar.

4 Bring the cream to the boil with the vanilla pod (scrape it to disperse the seeds) then simmer for three minutes.

5 Remove the cream from the heat, add the cinnamon and whisk.

6 Whisk together the cream, eggs and sugar.

7 Place most of the buttered croissant halves into a bowl and add the raisins.

8 Strain the custard mixture on to the croissants. Finish with the croissant tops and more custard.

9 Put the dish in a tray with hot water halfway up. Bake at 190C/Gas Mark 5 for 45 minutes until the custard is set.

10 Warm the jam and glaze the top of the pudding then sprinkle with a little icing sugar.

This dish also works well made with hot cross buns, brioche or stale white bread without the crusts.

This tipsy trifle is a special occasion dish but, as it's laced with plenty of alcohol, avoid having too many helpings if you're the one driving home! You can either serve it in individual glasses as we have here or pile it into one big bowl for traditional Sunday tea with the family.

Ingredients

Makes eight glasses or one large bowl

500ml whipping cream
500ml milk
300g sponge cake
1 jar plum, raspberry or strawberry jam
100g caster sugar
100g cornflour
4 egg yolks
1 vanilla pod
Splash brandy
1 dessertspoon cream sherry
200g apricots, fresh or tinned in light syrup
1 lemon
To decorate: griottine cherries in kirsch, grated chocolate, toasted almonds or fresh fruit

Step by step

1 Bring the milk to the boil with the vanilla pod and simmer for 10 minutes.

2 Put the egg yolks, half the sugar and the flour into a bowl and mix together thoroughly.

3 Remove the vanilla pod from the milk and pour on to the egg yolk mix. Gently simmer for three minutes then cool.

4 Drain the apricot halves and blend until smooth.

5 Whisk together the cream, lemon zest and juice, and the remaining sugar.

6 Break the sponge into cubes and place it in the base of the glasses.

7 Moisten the sponge with a little brandy.

8 Warm the jam then spoon this on top of the sponge pieces.

9 Add the sherry to the custard then leave to cool.

10 Layer the glass with custard, apricot purée and cream.

You can always go retro by sprinkling on hundreds and thousands or those 1970s-style silver balls!

This unusual ice cream goes nicely with chocolate and is a real treat on a sunny day. We made tubs of it for a party at Byfords Café, Deli and B&B in Holt held to celebrate the opening of their new rooms, and they served it in chocolate-coated cones which seemed to go down very well.

Ingredients

Serves four (freezable)

125ml Woodforde's Wherry bitter
250ml double cream
125g caster sugar
4 eggs

Step by step

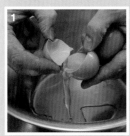

Separate the eggs.

Add 50g of the sugar to the egg yolks.

Whisk the egg yolks and sugar together until creamy.

Ensure the whisk is clean then whisk up the egg whites.

Add the remainder of the sugar to the egg whites and whisk again until they form soft peaks.

Whip the cream. When it is almost fully whipped, add the beer and continue whisking.

Fold the egg yolk mixture into the cream.

Add the egg whites.

Fold gently then place in a shallow container, cover with clingfilm and freeze overnight.

Serve in beer glasses or attractive dishes.

Woodforde's Wherry is a popular Norfolk beer but you don't usually see it as an ice cream!

Pumpkins are in season in the autumn and always make nice, colourful dishes. This is a traditional dessert in America during Thanksgiving, and is best served warm (you can use butternut squash instead of pumpkin). It goes well with maple syrup or maple syrup ice cream.

Ingredients

Makes a 20cm pie

For the pastry

250g plain flour
125g butter
50g icing sugar
1 egg

For the filling

1 medium-sized pumpkin
(approx 400g prepared weight)
75g soft, dark brown sugar
2 eggs and 1 extra egg yolk
½ teaspoon nutmeg
½ teaspoon Allspice
½ teaspoon ground ginger

Step by step

Make the pastry: Sieve together the icing sugar and plain flour then rub in the butter.

Break in the egg and mix to form a dough then roll this out on a floured board.

Line the flan tin with the pastry.

Make the filling: Peel and slice the pumpkin.

Place the pumpkin in a pan of boiling water and cook until just soft (around 10 minutes).

Drain and mash the pumpkin pieces.

Place the eggs and yolk into a bowl and whisk them together.

Place the cream into a saucepan and add the brown sugar, ginger, Allspice and nutmeg.

When the cream has boiled, pour it on to the eggs and mix well. Pour this on to the mashed pumpkin and stir well.

Pour the mixture into the pastry case and put it on a baking tray. Bake at 180C/Gas Mark 4 for 20 to 30 minutes.

The ingredients listed will make one large pumpkin pie or four smaller individual ones.

This is a lovely summer dessert. It works particularly well for barbecues because you can fill up the glasses in advance and then just add the scoops of ice cream or sorbet at the last minute. Its vibrant colour makes it very appealing and it makes a refreshing treat on balmy summer nights.

Ingredients

Serves four

2 large, fresh mangos or 2 tins of mangos in juice
200ml mango and apple juice
Four scoops good quality vanilla ice cream
or mango sorbet
50g caster sugar
1 small piece root ginger
Juice and zest of 1 lime
Handful mint leaves

Step by step

Peel the mangos.

Dice a quarter of the fruit and set aside; place the rest in a jug or bowl.

Peel and slice the ginger then add this to the jug.

Add the lime juice and zest and stir well.

Add the caster sugar.

Pour in the mango and apple juice.

Blend the mango mixture until smooth.

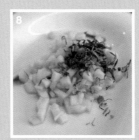

Chop a handful of mint leaves and mix these with the mango dice.

Divide the mango mixture into attractive glasses and top with the mint and mango dice.

Place a scoop of ice cream or sorbet on top of each glass followed by more mango dice and fresh mint leaves.

Mango and apple juice works well but you can also use orange, pineapple or passion fruit juice.

Norfolk is famous for its lavender and it goes perfectly with peaches. The dried lavender flowers in this dish lend the peaches an unusual, exotic flavour; you can serve them with some scoops of decent vanilla ice cream and some raspberry purée to make an upmarket peach melba.

Ingredients

Serves four

6 ripe peaches
1 teaspoon dried lavender flowers
1 teaspoon green peppercorns
Knob butter
100g granulated sugar
Few fresh bay leaves
Few sprigs fresh thyme
Splash peach schnapps

Step by step

1 Make a cross on the top of each peach with a sharp knife.

2 Place the peaches in boiling water and blanch them for 10 seconds.

3 Take the fruit off the heat, remove the peel then slice each peach in half.

4 Melt a knob of butter in a frying pan.

5 Add the peaches.

6 Cover the peaches with the sugar.

7 Sprinkle on the dried lavender flowers.

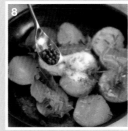

8 Add the bay leaves, thyme and dried peppercorns.

9 Shake the mixture over the peaches then roast them in the oven at 200C/Gas Mark 6 for 20 minutes.

10 Remove the peaches from the heat, add the schnapps then return to the heat to warm through before serving.

A heavy-bottomed frying pan that can be placed in an oven is a useful tool for this dish.

Thanks to the ground almonds, this lovely cake is gluten-free so is fine for those who can't eat wheat. The longer you keep it, the more moist it becomes so you can serve it as a cake when you first make it or keep it for a little longer and then serve it as an orange and almond pudding instead.

Ingredients

Makes eight to 10 portions (freezable)

2 large oranges

250g caster sugar

300g ground almonds

2 teaspoons baking powder
(gluten-free if required)

½ teaspoon Allspice

5 medium-sized eggs

Step by step

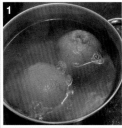

1 Simmer the oranges in a pan of boiling water for 20 minutes.

2 Remove the oranges from the pan and cut them into quarters, leaving the peel on.

3 Place the fruit into a food processor and purée until smooth.

4 Put the sugar into a bowl then add the eggs.

5 Whisk the eggs and sugar together.

6 Add the ground almonds and baking powder then whisk the mixture again.

7 Beat in the Allspice.

8 Fold in the orange pulp.

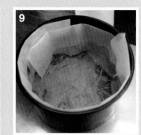

9 Line a cake tin with greased greaseproof paper.

10 Spoon in the cake mix and bake at 180C/Gas Mark 4 for 45 minutes.

This cake uses the whole fruit and is delicious hot or cold. If you haven't got Allspice, use cinnamon.

This dish gets so many positive comments at The Lavender House that it's the only thing that's always on the menu. Also, as I have such a sweet tooth, I absolutely love it! The parfait not only looks good but the great thing is that it's very simple to prepare.

Ingredients

Serves four (freezable)

For the parfait
160g peanut butter
150ml whipping or double cream
50g sugar
2 large eggs

For the caramel
100ml single cream
50g butter
50g sugar

To serve
Brandy snap cases
Handful mini marshmallows

Step by step

1. Separate the eggs and place the yolks in a bowl with the sugar.

2. Place the bowl over a pan of hot water and whisk the egg yolks and sugar together.

3. Whisk the cream until it forms soft peaks.

4. Gently fold the peanut butter into the cream.

5. Whisk the egg whites. Fold the egg yolk and sugar mixture into the cream, followed by the egg whites.

6. Pour the mixture into individual ramekins or espresso cups. Freeze for at least three hours.

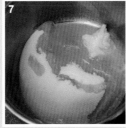

7. **Make the caramel:** Slowly heat the butter and sugar together in a pan.

8. Take the mixture off the heat and add the cream.

9. Return to the heat and bring it back to the boil.

10. Place the parfait in the brandy snap case. Decorate with the caramel, the sauce and the mini marshmallows.

For fruit parfaits, keep the quantities the same and swap the peanut butter for thick fruit purée.

Hand-made in your own kitchen, there is little to beat a fresh lemon tart. Eat it on the day you bake it to best experience the melt-in-the-mouth pastry and the sharp citrus cream filling. This dish is equally at home when served with morning coffee as it is gracing a glamorous dinner party table.

Ingredients

Makes a 23cm tart

For the pastry

250g plain flour
140g soft butter
50g icing sugar
Zest of ½ lemon
1 egg yolk
Pinch salt
Cold water to bind

For the filling

5 medium eggs
80g caster sugar
90ml double cream
Juice of 3 lemons
Zest of ½ lemon

Step by step

Make the pastry: Place all the pastry ingredients into a food processor and pulse until combined.

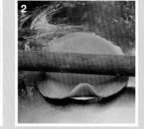

Roll the pastry out on a floured surface then line the flan tin.

Push the edges of the pastry down, raise the sides and remove the surplus then leave it to rest for 15 minutes.

Cover the pastry with greaseproof paper, fill it with baking beans or rice and bake at 180C/ Gas Mark 4.

Cook until the pastry has set (around 10 minutes) then brush the inside with a little beaten egg white.

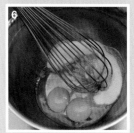

Reduce the oven to 170C/Gas Mark 3.
Make the filling: Whisk the eggs and sugar together.

Whisk the cream then combine with the egg and sugar mixture.

Chop the lemon zest and squeeze the juice. Add these to the cream.

Pour the mixture into the pastry case then bake for around 30 minutes until set.

Allow the tart to cool completely then dust it with icing sugar and caramelise it using a blowtorch.

Try serving this with a few poached blackcurrants, a handful of raspberries or some crème fraîche.

These delicious fruit tarts confirm that summer is really here. Get out and about to your nearest farm shop, roadside stall or Pick Your Own then rustle up this fabulous combination - succulent Norfolk strawberries, perfectly crisp pastry and cold Continental custard.

Ingredients

Serves four

For the pastry
500g plain flour
250g butter
150g icing sugar
1 egg
Cold water to bind

For the filling
500ml milk
75g caster sugar
50g cornflour
4 egg yolks
1 vanilla pod
Dash Amaretto

To serve
2 punnets strawberries
2 dessertspoons apricot jam

Step by step

Blend all the pastry ingredients in a food processor until the dough binds then push together till smooth.

Roll the pastry out on a floured surface.

Make the filling: Whisk together the egg yolks, caster sugar and cornflour.

Place the vanilla pod into the milk, bring this to the boil then pour it slowly into the egg mixture and whisk.

Bring back up to the boil, whisking continuously. Add the Amaretto then strain and cool.

Place the pastry in the flan cases, raising the edges until they stand proud of the rim then prick them with a fork.

Line the flan cases with greaseproof paper and baking beans. Bake at 180C/Gas Mark 4 until set (about 10 minutes).

Remove the baking beans then return the flan cases to the oven until golden brown (around 10 minutes).

Spoon the cool cream filling into the flan cases and top with some sliced strawberries.

Glaze with apricot jam.

These delicious tarts remind me of France, but now you can recreate them in your own home.

This is an easy recipe to make without an ice cream machine. If you're using forced rhubarb the sorbet should be a nice bright pink colour but if you use the home-grown variety you might like to add a pinch of red food colouring to ensure that it has a rosy pink glow.

Ingredients

Serves four (freezable)

250g rhubarb
250g granulated sugar
250ml water
1 glass white or rosé wine
3 slices fresh ginger
Juice and zest of 1 lemon

To serve
Few teaspoons icing sugar
Few leaves fresh mint

Step by step

Pour the sugar and water into a pan.

Add the lemon zest and lemon juice.

Chop the rhubarb and add it to the liquid along with the sugar.

Add the ginger.

Simmer until the rhubarb is just cooked (around three minutes).

Leave the rhubarb mixture to cool, keeping a little for decoration.

Add the wine.

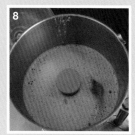

Blitz the mixture in a food processor for a few minutes then place it in a bowl and freeze overnight.

Remove the sorbet and break it up with a spoon then blend it again in the food processor. Freeze for two hours.

Place into pretty dishes. Decorate with fresh mint and perhaps a little icing sugar.

If you want to try something a little more exotic, you can replace the ginger with lemon grass.

Every chef has a favourite recipe. This one has all the prerequisite qualities – it is easy to prepare, looks fantastic and, most importantly, tastes great. Hopefully it'll become a staple recipe in your home, just as it is at The Lavender House, although we like it to look more dainty!

Ingredients

Makes a 24cm cheesecake (freezable)

125g fresh raspberries
250g mascarpone or soft cream cheese
250ml whipping or double cream
125g white chocolate
100g icing sugar
125g butter
1 large packet chocolate chip cookies, crushed
Eau de framboise or any other liqueur (optional)
Juice of ½ lemon

Step by step

Melt the butter then add the cookies. Mix well then press into a 24cm spring-loaded cake tin.

Crush half the raspberries with half the icing sugar, the lemon juice and a tot of liqueur.

Place the white chocolate in a bowl and melt it gently over hot water, stirring continuously.

Whisk the cream until it forms a soft peak.

Whisk together the cream cheese and the rest of the sugar.

Fold together the cream cheese, cream, most of the remaining whole raspberries and the melted white chocolate.

Put the mixture on top of the biscuit base followed by the crushed raspberries then repeat.

Smooth the top and tap the sides of the tin. Leave to set in the fridge for three hours.

Loosen the cheesecake with a palette knife.

Dust with some sieved icing sugar and decorate with the remaining raspberries.

You can swap the raspberries for strawberries, rhubarb or blackberries – whatever is in season.

Sweet things

We've called this section "Sweet things" rather than petits fours because, although most of these items go well with coffee, many of them are just as good on their own. And if you've got a special occasion coming up - a birthday, anniversary or Christmas get-together, for instance, you could always make boxes of these sweets, biscuits and treats for presents. The following recipes represent just a small selection of Julia Hetherton's talented handiwork; for more delicious offerings you'll just have to come and see us! Looking forward to welcoming you to The Lavender House, Anna Sewell House Restaurant or The Pigs pub for lunch, dinner or a cookery class soon. Meanwhile, enjoy!

Honey Madeleines

Use a Madeleine tray for these biscuits to achieve that well-known shape. These come in metal and rubber, but the rubber ones work best as the biscuits are easier to remove from these. The Madeleines keep well in an airtight container or you can freeze them and use them at a later date.

Ingredients

Makes 40 small Madeleines or 20 large ones (freezable)

90g plain flour
90g melted butter
75g granulated sugar
50g honey
1 tablespoon soft brown sugar
1 teaspoon baking powder
2 eggs
1 tablespoon icing sugar

Step by step

1 Break the eggs into a bowl.

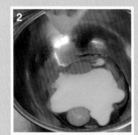

2 Add the granulated sugar.

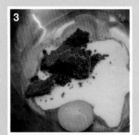

3 Add the brown sugar.

4 Whisk the mixture until pale and creamy (around five minutes).

5 Add the plain flour and the baking powder.

6 With a metal spoon, fold the flour and baking powder into the eggs and sugar.

7 Once the mixture is half-folded, add half the melted butter and fold this in, followed by the rest of the butter.

8 Add the honey and fold the mixture again.

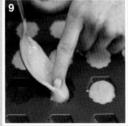

9 Place spoonfuls of the mixture into a Madeleine tin. Bake at 220C/Gas Mark 8 for five minutes for small Madeleines or 10 for bigger ones.

10 Remove the biscuits from the oven and leave them to cool in the tray. When cool, take them out and dust them with icing sugar.

Using a metal spoon to fold in the dry ingredients helps as this cuts into the mixture more effectively.

160 www.thelavenderhouse.co.uk

This recipe can be very useful as you can keep the dough in the fridge for a couple of weeks and then just use it to make some cookies when you need them, so that you've always got freshly baked biscuits to hand. You can also make mini cookies to go with after-dinner coffee.

Ingredients

Makes 20 (freezable)

175g self-raising flour
115g caster sugar
90g butter
50g dark chocolate chips
1 egg

Step by step

Put the butter and sugar into a bowl and cream them together.

Break in the egg and beat well.

Add the flour and the chocolate chips.

Mix together to form a soft dough.

Divide the mixture in two.

Roll each half into a sausage shape.

Wrap these in clingfilm then refrigerate for a few minutes.

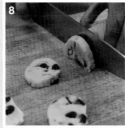

With a sharp knife, cut the cookie dough into biscuits that are about 2cm thick.

Place these on a greased baking tray.

Bake at 180C/Gas Mark 4 until golden brown (around 10 minutes).

You might need to re-shape the biscuits a little with your hands when you cut the dough into cookies.

At The Lavender House we serve mini marshmallows with the iced peanut butter parfait (see the recipe in the desserts section). You can also roll the marshmallow in coconut to give it more texture, or add a teaspoon of desiccated coconut to the marshmallow mixture.

Ingredients

Makes at least 24 pieces

100g caster sugar
100ml water
1 ripe banana
2 egg whites
1 ½ leaves gelatine
Juice of ½ lemon
1 dessertspoon icing sugar

Step by step

1 Place the sugar and water in a pan.

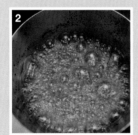

2 Put the pan on the hob and bring the mixture up to the boil. Boil until it becomes a thick syrup.

3 Soak the gelatine in water until soft (around five minutes).

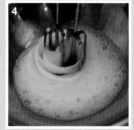

4 Using an electric whisk, whisk the egg whites until they form peaks.

5 Take the sugar syrup off the heat and whisk this into the egg whites.

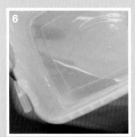

6 Take the gelatine out of the water and melt this in the microwave for 15 seconds.

7 Pour the gelatine into the egg white and sugar mixture and whisk until it begins to cool.

8 Mash the banana with a fork and add this and the lemon juice to the egg whites. Whisk again until combined.

9 Line a deep tray with clingfilm and pour the mixture into the tray.

10 Cover the tray with clingfilm and place it in the fridge for four hours then cut the marshmallow out with a cutter or sharp knife.

If you have got an electric whisk, it's worthwhile using it for this as it'll stop your arm aching!

Fudge is very flexible – you can use other chocolate and nuts for this if you prefer, put coffee through it, or add rum and raisins or vanilla. The chocolate helps with the smoothness of the fudge as without it it can be rather grainy. It also helps the mixture to set quickly.

Ingredients

Makes 24 squares

350g white chocolate chips
350g caster sugar
150ml evaporated milk
50g pistachios
Good pinch salt

Step by step

Place the evaporated milk in a heavy-based saucepan.

Add the sugar and salt.

Bring the mixture to the boil, stirring continuously. Lower the heat and simmer gently, stirring, for five minutes.

Remove the pan from the heat and add the white chocolate.

Add the pistachios and stir the mixture gently with a metal spoon until the chocolate has completely melted.

Grease a 20cm square cake tin or line it with baking paper.

Pour the mixture into the tin.

Use a palette knife to spread the mixture out evenly.

Cover with clingfilm then leave to set in the fridge for a couple of hours.

Take out of the fridge and leave for a few minutes then cut into squares.

This will keep in an airtight container for a couple of weeks with greaseproof paper between the layers.

Coconut tuiles

These coconut tuiles go very well with soft desserts such as cheesecake, ice cream and sorbets as they add some crunch. The best way to make them is to shape them over a rolling pin while they're soft and then leave them to set; they'll become very crisp as they cool.

Ingredients

Makes at least 24

50g plain flour
50g butter
50g caster sugar
50ml egg white
25g desiccated coconut

Step by step

Place the butter in a bowl.

Add the sugar.

Cream these together.

Add the flour.

Add the egg white.

Add the coconut.

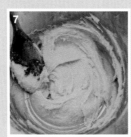

Mix well.

Place teaspoons of the mixture on to a greased baking tray or baking mat and spread them out to form circles.

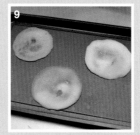

Bake for three to four minutes at 180C/Gas Mark 4.

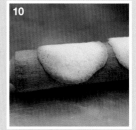

Remove the biscuits from the oven and place them over a rolling pin. Leave them to set for a few minutes then remove and cool.

If the biscuits harden before you have a chance to roll them, simply soften them again in the oven.

This is incredibly easy to make so if friends come round at short notice, why not give it a try? It is also a good recipe for children as they can have fun making all sorts of different-shaped biscuits. Use sugar rather than flour when rolling out as flour will spoil the consistency.

Ingredients

Makes around 20 biscuits (freezable)

150g plain flour
50g caster sugar
100g butter
25g caster sugar for rolling out
Icing sugar for dusting

Step by step

Place the flour in a bowl.

Add the sugar.

Add the butter.

Rub in the butter until the mixture forms a dough.

Sprinkle the caster sugar on a clean surface.

Use a rolling pin to roll out the dough until it's about 10mm thick.

Using a pastry cutter, cut the dough into biscuit shapes.

Gently lift the biscuits with a palette knife and place them on a greased baking tray.

Prick the biscuits with a fork, sprinkle a little more sugar on top then place them in an oven at 180C/Gas Mark 4 for five minutes.

Remove the biscuits from the tray and place them on a cooling rack. Dust with icing sugar.

Just cook the biscuits until they're slightly golden as you don't want them to go too brown.

This is a quick and easy dish but please be very careful when making it as the water and sugar will become very hot indeed. The hazelnut brittle goes very well with coffee or you can crumble it up and serve it with ice cream. Peanuts and pecans also work well with this.

Ingredients

Serves four

100g hazelnuts
200g granulated sugar
100ml water
Squeeze lemon juice

Step by step

1 Spread the hazelnuts out on a baking tray and place them in the oven at 180C/Gas Mark 4 for a few minutes.

2 When toasted, leave the hazelnuts to cool then rub them between the palms of your hands to remove the skins.

3 Place the hazelnuts in a bowl and crush them with a rolling pin.

4 Pour the sugar into a pan and add enough water to cover it.

5 Put the pan on the hob and boil the mixture rapidly until it caramelises - don't stir it!

6 When the mixture starts to colour, squeeze in the lemon juice.

7 Plunge the pan into a tray of cold water to cool it down quickly.

8 Pour the hazelnuts into the water and sugar mixture and stir well.

9 Lightly grease a baking tray with butter. Spread the mixture out over the baking tray then refrigerate for a few minutes.

10 When set, break the brittle into small pieces and serve.

Plunging the pan of water and sugar into cold water will prevent the mixture cooking any further.

I have no idea why these are called "brandy snaps" when they don't contain any brandy, but you could always mix some brandy into the whipped cream before you serve them if you like. They go well with ice cream, sorbets and fresh fruit or simply served on their own with real coffee.

Ingredients

Makes 24 brandy snaps

50g butter
50g golden syrup
50g demerera sugar
50g plain flour
½ teaspoon ground ginger
½ teaspoon lemon juice

Step by step

Put the butter into a pan.

Add the demerara sugar.

Warm the golden syrup in the microwave for a few seconds then add it to the butter and sugar.

Place the mixture on the hob until the butter and sugar have dissolved. Stir well.

Remove the pan from the heat and add the flour. Whisk until smooth.

Add the ground ginger and the lemon juice.

Place four teaspoons of the mixture at a time on to greased baking trays or silicone mats.

Bake at 160C/Gas Mark 3 until golden in colour (about six minutes).

Allow the brandy snaps to cool slightly before rolling them around a wooden spoon and keep them there until the snaps harden.

Serve with fresh fruit, ice cream or whipped cream.

Warming the golden syrup in the microwave before adding it to the mixture will make it easier to use.

Tiffin is a non-baked, set, sweet snack whose base is made from biscuits, butter, golden syrup and sugar. It's incredibly rich so just have a little at a time as I don't want to be held responsible for expanding waistlines! It goes very well with tea and coffee.

Ingredients

Makes at least 12 pieces

200g cooking chocolate (half milk and half dark)
200g Rich Tea biscuits
100g butter
4 teaspoons cocoa
2 tablespoons golden syrup
2 tablespoons caster sugar
1 glass brandy
Handful raisins
Handful prunes

Step by step

Put the golden syrup, butter, sugar and cocoa powder into a pan.

Place the pan on the hob until the mixture melts then remove it from the heat.

Crush the biscuits.

Add the prunes and raisins to the chocolate mixture.

Pour in the brandy.

Add the crushed biscuits and mix well.

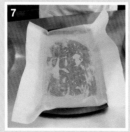

Line a Swiss roll tin or shallow baking tray with greaseproof paper.

Pour the mixture into the tin and press down.

Melt the chocolate in the microwave, mix well then pour this over the top of the biscuit mix.

Spread the chocolate with a palette knife then place the tiffin in the fridge until set (about an hour). Cut into squares.

This is one of our favourite recipes for children who are discovering cooking for the first time.

www.thelavenderhouse.co.uk

We make hundreds of these at The Lavender House. As they have cream in them, refrigerate them and use them within two weeks. You can use Kahlua or Grand Marnier instead of Baileys, and remember to leave plenty of time for them to set; at least two hours.

Ingredients

Makes about 40 truffles

300g dark chocolate chips
200g cocoa powder
50ml Baileys
100ml whipping or double cream
50g butter

Step by step

1 Pour the cream into a saucepan.

2 Add the Baileys.

3 Bring the mixture to the boil.

4 Once boiled, take the mixture off the heat and add the chocolate chips.

5 Using a whisk, stir the mixture gently until the chocolate has melted.

6 Add the butter and stir until smooth.

7 Line a tray at least 2cm deep with clingfilm. Pour the chocolate mixture into the tray.

8 Place the tray in the fridge until the mixture has set.

9 Remove from the fridge and the tin and, using a sharp knife, cut the chocolate into squares then cut each square in half diagonally.

10 Roll the truffles in cocoa powder and place them on a serving dish.

Try adding nuts to the mixture or for rum and raisin truffles swap the Baileys for rum.

Contents

Photographer: Keiron Tovell

www.keirontovell.com

Keiron Tovell is a popular freelance photographer who has a wealth of experience behind the lens. For many years he worked full-time for the Eastern Daily Press and then became the dedicated photographer for the monthly glossy magazine, EDP Norfolk.

Since embarking on his own, Keiron has built up an enviable client list including Richard Hughes' restaurants and a number of other well-known Norfolk restaurants and hotels. As Keiron says: "I'm very keen on cooking and particularly enjoy food photography so it was a pleasure to take all the shots for this book. I've known Richard Hughes for several years and he is great to work with. I enjoy the atmosphere of a professional kitchen, watching the chefs at work and seeing what goes into producing the finished dishes, so this has been a great experience." Keiron is married to Cat and they live in Norwich with their dog Finn.

Editor: Carolyn Bowden

carolynbowden@btinternet.com

Carolyn Bowden has lived in Norfolk for around five years after coming up to the county from London. She used to edit the EDP Norfolk magazine, and before this was a features writer for The Daily Express Saturday magazine. Today Carolyn is a freelance writer and also assists Richard Hughes and his business partner, Iain Wilson, with the publicity and marketing for their five businesses: The Lavender House Restaurant & Cookery School in Brundall; the Anna Sewell House Restaurant in Great Yarmouth; The Pigs pub in Edgefield; Byfords Café, Deli and B&B in Holt; and The King's Head pub, also in Holt.

Carolyn lives in Norwich with her partner, Miles, and their little boy, James. As she says: "Miles and I are both keen on cooking and we must have every cookery book and kitchen gadget under the sun! I have really enjoyed working with Richard Hughes and Keiron Tovell on this book as it's given me a real insight into how a restaurant works, and watching Richard make each dish has inspired me to try making some of the dishes at home."